I Have Called You Friends

I Have Called You Friends

Reflections on Reconciliation

~

IN HONOR OF

Frank T. Griswold

Cowley Publications
CAMBRIDGE, MASSACHUSETTS

Published in the United States of America by Cowley Publications,
a division of the Society of Saint John the Evangelist. No portion of
this book may be reproduced, stored in or introduced into a retrieval
system, or transmitted, in any form or by any means—including
photocopying—without the prior written permission of Cowley
Publications, except in the case of brief quotations embedded in
critical articles and reviews.

Library of Congress Cataloging-in-Publication Data

I have called you friends : reflections on reconciliation in honor of
Frank T. Griswold.
     p.   cm.
   Includes bibliographical references.
   ISBN-10: 1-56101-248-3   ISBN-13: 978-1-56101-248-0
   (pbk. : alk. paper)
     1. Reconciliation—Religious aspects—Christianity.
   2. Reconciliation—Religious aspects—Episcopal Church.
   I. Griswold, Frank T., 1937–   II. Braver, Barbara Leix, 1938–
     BT738.27.I2   2006
     234'.5—dc22   2006000483

Back cover photo: Anne Wetzel
Cover design: Kyle G. Hunter
Interior design: Wendy Holdman

This book was printed in Canada on acid-free paper.

Cowley Publications
4 Brattle Street
Cambridge, Massachusetts 02138
800-225-1534 • www.cowley.org

Contents

Contributors

Denise M. Ackermann is Extraordinary Professor of Christian Theology at the University of Stellenbosch in South Africa.

Curtis G. Almquist, SSJE is the Superior of the Society of Saint John the Evangelist, serving at the Society's monastery in Cambridge, Massachusetts.

Michael Battle is Associate Dean for Academic Affairs and Vice President of Virginia Theological Seminary in Alexandria, Virginia.

William Danaher is Associate Professor of Theology and Christian Ethics at the University of the South in Sewanee, Tennessee.

Ellen F. Davis is Professor of Bible and Practical Theology at Duke Divinity School, Duke University, in Durham, North Carolina.

Esther de Waal has written and spoken extensively primarily on the monastic tradition. She lives on the Welsh borders and spends each winter as scholar-in-residence at the Cathedral College in Washington, D.C.

Ian T. Douglas is the Angus Dun Professor of Mission and World Christianity at Episcopal Divinity School in Cambridge, Massachusetts.

Brian J. Grieves is Director of Peace and Justice Ministries for the Episcopal Church.

John Haughey, SJ is Professor of Religious Ethics at Loyola University, Chicago, and a senior research fellow at Woodstock Theological Center, Georgetown University.

Peter S. Hawkins is Professor of Religion and Director of the Luce Program in Scripture and the Literary Arts at Boston University.

Martha Horne is the Dean and President of Virginia Theological Seminary, Alexandria, Virginia.

Cynthia Briggs Kittredge is the Ernest J. Villavaso, Jr. Associate Professor of New Testament at the Episcopal Theological Seminary of the Southwest in Austin, Texas.

Peter James Lee is the Bishop of Virginia and served as the co-chair of the committee to nominate the twenty-sixth Presiding Bishop.

Mark A. McIntosh is Associate Professor of Theology at Loyola University Chicago and canon theologian to the Presiding Bishop.

Margaret R. Miles is Emerita Professor of Historical Theology at the Graduate Theological Union in Berkeley, California.

Esther Mombo is Academic Dean of St. Paul's United Theological College in Limuru, Kenya.

Njongonkulu Ndungane is Archbishop of Cape Town and Primate of the Anglican Church of Southern Africa.

Luci Shaw, the author of numerous books of prose and poetry, is Writer-in-Residence and Lecturer at Regent College in Vancouver, British Columbia, Canada.

M. Thomas Shaw, SSJE is the Bishop of Massachusetts.

Jenny Te Paa is Principal of Te Rau Kahikatea, The College of St. John the Evangelist, in Auckland, New Zealand.

Kathryn Tanner is the Dorothy Grant Maclear Professor of Theology in the Divinity School at the University of Chicago.

Desmond Tutu is Archbishop Emeritus of Cape Town, South Africa.

Louis Weil is the Hodges-Haynes Professor of Liturgics at the Church Divinity School of the Pacific in Berkeley, California.

George L. W. Werner is the thirty-first President of the House of Deputies.

Rowan Williams is the Archbishop of Canterbury.

J. Robert Wright is the St. Mark's-in-the-Bowery Professor of Ecclesiastical History at General Theological Seminary, New York, and is the historiographer of the Episcopal Church.

Preface

THE IDEA FOR A FESTSCHRIFT as a way of honoring the twenty-fifth Presiding Bishop of the Episcopal Church arrived in a moment of grace, and thus came with a sense of rightness. It happened like this. A group was seated around a dinner table at Camp Allen in Texas during the meeting of the House of Bishops in March 2005. We ate and talked, moving around many subjects of common interest, as conversations in such settings most often do. Then, someone asked: *What are we going to do to honor Frank at the end of his term?* The conversation continued with energy and various thoughts—some plausible and others quite hilarious—came forward. We quickly agreed that how the Presiding Bishop might be honored and celebrated deserved careful thought, and that whatever was done should be very right for him. We were also very clear that an evening of laudatory reminiscences launched by his fifth-grade teacher and moving sweetly forward, chapter by chapter, most definitely wouldn't do.

It was then that I heard myself saying "Something like a festschrift." *Festschrift.* This word does not often drop from my lips, but I saw others nodding in agreement and within just a moment or two there was a sense around the table that we had the nub of an idea. Who could imagine we would pose the question and come to resolution so easily? Ah, the grace that was in it. Thus, over Camp Allen's fried chicken, the thought sprang forth, and the next steps suggested themselves.

It seemed at that moment as if it would be my task to give this idea further shape and encourage this project on its way, given that I had served in the Office of the Presiding Bishop through all of Frank Griswold's primacy. As it turned out, the idea didn't need a great deal of encouragement, but rather grew and developed as if each step had a certain inevitability. First there was the question of the theme. Over these past nine years the Presiding Bishop has taught about reconciliation: conversation, conversion, communion—all grounded in Jesus' meeting us in all our particularities and isolation and calling us into the ever greater friendship of the Holy Spirit. Thus, it was immediately apparent that the essayists should focus, each in their own way, on the theme of reconciliation and our participation in what God has already accomplished through Christ.

A book needs a publisher. Because Bishop Griswold's relationship with the Society of St. John the Evangelist reaches back to his days as a student at St. Paul's School, Cowley Publications was my first call. The response was immediate and positive, and everyone at Cowley who has been part of this festschrift has contributed with creativity and enthusiasm.

Each person I approached to be part of this collection accepted not only with alacrity, but with joy: they were grateful for an opportunity to honor Frank Griswold through their own offerings, and to further the enterprise of theological reflection. And thus it went, from a question over dinner to this handsome volume, pushed along on a stream of grace.

Everyone who has been part of *I Have Called You Friends* so wants this book of essays to be a gift to the church and a contribution to our conversation, our conversion, our communion, and to our living the reconciled life already given to us through Christ. And we hope and pray—as I trust our readers will as well—that this volume will be a proper and loving gift to one who has served as the overseer of the Episcopal Church as our teacher and as our friend.

Barbara Braver
Editor

I Have Called You Friends

The Magnanimity
of Reconciliation

Desmond Tutu

A Mother's Outburst

Just recently I read in one of our South African newspapers what a mother said to the man who killed her only
child. She hoped that he would be sentenced to a very
long term in prison, indeed that he would never leave the
prison and that he would rot forever in hell afterwards.
We are not usually shocked at such harsh and bitter sen-
timents because we believe that is how a normal human
being reacts to an outrage such as the slaying of an only
child. We regard it as the expected normal thing. Thus we
realize that forgiving is not cheap, is not easy.

The Magnanimity of Jesus

Then we come face to face with a remarkable incident.
On that first Good Friday outside Jerusalem, Jesus was
being nailed to the cross, condemned to suffer an ex-
cruciating death in a gross miscarriage of justice. This
young man who out of sheer exhaustion could sleep
soundly even in the midst of a raging storm on the lake,
who was filled with a deep anguish at the prospect of

death and sought the solace and presence of his close associates—in short, someone of flesh and blood as you and I, truly human as we are, well, this young man prayed, "Father forgive them for they know not what they are doing." We would have expected him to be flailing about in the agony of the nailing, experiencing unbearable pain and what is more undeserved suffering and that he would give his tormentors a tongue-lashing. It is mind-boggling that instead of excoriating them he should actually be praying for them in an extraordinary exhibition of magnanimity, of generosity of spirit, not intent on giving as good as he had gotten.

Perhaps we have heard the biblical accounts so often that the wonder of Jesus' reaction to his suffering no longer strikes us as odd. It could well be that we needed to be shocked out of our being blasé by something like the disturbing brutality and violence of Mel Gibson's film *The Passion of the Christ*. What happened on that Good Friday was no Sunday school picnic for the squeamish. It was for real and it was ghastly. Improbably, it was out of that ghastliness and brutality that Jesus spoke so magnanimously, acted with such a mind-boggling generosity of spirit to set in train the God project of reconciling all things to God. Humanly speaking, Jesus should have been cursing and consigning his tormentors to the perdition that most of his supporters believed they deserved.

Mandela's Magnanimity

The miracle of South Africa's relatively peaceful transition from apartheid's repression to the freedom of democracy was in large measure due to a decision to follow the path of reconciliation rather than retribution and revenge, to seek to forgive rather than to pay back in the same coin. God was so good as to have given us a Nelson Mandela at this crucial moment in our history. Of course we must not discount the critical role played by Mr. F. W. de Klerk. Had his intransigent predecessor remained in power it is almost certain that we would not have made it to a negotiated settlement. So we must give Mr. de Klerk the credit due to him.

But it is equally certain that Mr. de Klerk's courageous initiatives of 1990 would have come to nothing had Nelson Mandela been different. He amazed nearly everyone after twenty-seven years of incarceration in what most would agree had been a gross miscarriage of justice. Nobody would have been surprised had he emerged consumed with bitterness, baying for the blood of his tormentors and the oppressors of his people. Most would have said, "That's to be expected. That's how most human beings would after all react." He surprised everyone with his amazing magnanimity, which called not for revenge but for reconciliation, not for retaliation but for forgiveness. No one could accuse him of speaking glibly about forgiveness. After all, if they had challenged his credentials he could say, "twenty-seven years," and that would silence any who might have wanted to be his detractors. His suffering gave him a credibility and an authority very difficult to obtain in any other way. After his election as South Africa's first democratically elected President, he invited his former white jailer to attend his Presidential inauguration as a V.I.P. guest of the new President. One of the first guests to a Presidential lunch was Dr. Percy Yutar, who had been the Prosecutor in the Rivonia Trial when Mandela and his African National Congress colleagues were given life sentences. Dr. Yutar had sought the death penalty. This was how Nelson Mandela advanced the cause of reconciliation, not just by precept but more tellingly by example. He lived out eloquently the magnanimity that promoted reconciliation, and he it was who appointed South Africa's Truth and Reconciliation Commission (TRC).

The Victim's Magnanimity

During the sessions of the TRC we were frequently bowled over by the magnanimity, the nobility, and generosity of spirit of those who by rights should have been bristling with resentment and anger and who should have been claiming their pound of flesh but were doing nothing of the sort. They awed us by their willingness to forgive the perpetrators of some of the most gruesome atrocities, and even on occasion to embrace publicly those who had visited so much suffering on them.

One such was Mrs. Savage, who had survived a hand-grenade attack on a golf club Christmas dinner party by one of the liberation movements, the Pan African Congress. She was so badly injured that she spent six months in an intensive care unit and when she was discharged from hospital needed her children to help her bathe, clothe, and eat. She still had shrapnel in her and could not walk through a security checkpoint without setting off the alarms. She said of the experience that had left her in such a dire condition that it had enriched her life. And while we were still recovering she went on to say that she wanted to meet the perpetrator in a spirit of forgiveness. She wanted to forgive him for his dastardly deed, and then she added quite breathtakingly, "I want to ask him to forgive me." Unbelievable—what moral stature!

I would sometimes stop the proceedings of the Commission after moments such as these. I would observe that we were in the presence of something holy and that we really ought to take off our shoes, for we were standing on holy ground.

The Presiding Bishop's Magnanimity

When the Anglican Communion was rocked by the fallout from the consecration of Bishop Gene Robinson a lot of heat was generated in the often-unedifying exchanges between those supporting or those condemning that step by the Episcopal Church. To have said, "How these Christians love one another," could now only have been as a mocking jibe and not, as originally, in admiration.

I was deeply impressed by how irenic the Presiding Bishop, Frank Griswold, was in his utterances and how magnanimous he and the House of Bishops were in graciously accepting the request to have ECUSA recuse itself from the Anglican Consultative Council until the next Lambeth Conference. It may well turn out to be Bishop Frank's finest hour. It has been the same generosity of spirit, the magnanimity, that our Lord revealed at the crucifixion. It is of the same order as that of a Nelson Mandela and of the many who came to testify before the TRC.

May this spirit imbue all in our Communion.
God bless this good and faithful servant, Frank
Griswold, and his beloved Phoebe.

Taste and See

Ellen F. Davis

THESE REFLECTIONS DRAW UPON and connect two parts of Scripture that are central to Frank Griswold's life and ministry: the psalms, which he prays daily in both the Office and the Eucharistic liturgy, and the letters of Paul, which have been and remain foundational for his own formation as a theologian—like Paul, a learned theologian whose theological thinking develops mostly in direct response to questions and problems encountered "on the ground," in the daily life of the church.

The psalms are daily prayers in the truest sense. None is a prayer for every occasion. Rather, one by one, the psalms capture in words the varying and vacillating moods in which people who pray every day necessarily come before God. I note here that we customarily speak as though these prayers came from a single person, for they represent the corporate mind and heart of Israel. The mood of the "psalmist" may shift from prayer to prayer, and even within a single prayer. Yet at the same time, they speak to and of a God whom the psalmist often calls "my Rock" (Ps. 18:2, 46; 19:14, etc.). From the experience of God's rocklike steadiness—God's steadiness *for us*—comes the ability and the desire to "bless

YHWH[1] at all times." The Presiding Bishop's ministry bespeaks his own trust in God's steadiness, and the daily renewal of his praise. This meditation on Psalm 34 is offered in thanksgiving for that ministry.

~

An Arabic proverb sums up all human experience thus:

One day for you, one day against you.

A well-known religious teaching amplifies the proverb:

When time is for you, give thanks to God.
And when it is against you, have patience, endure.[2]

That wisdom comes from seventh-century Arabia, but it might as well have come from ancient Israel, because it exactly captures the thought of our psalm. In the terms of the Arabic proverb, the psalmist is speaking on a good day, when things are for him. So he begins by giving thanks to God:

I will bless YHWH at all times;
his praise shall ever be in my mouth. (v. 2)

But as you read through the psalm, it is evident that the poet-teacher who wrote it has an eye to the second day, the day that is against us. Our psalmist, it turns out, is someone well acquainted with trouble. And so he offers expert instruction for how to cope with that second day when it comes, as inevitably it will, again and again to each of us, in our individual lives and in the life we share in Christ Jesus.

Most psalms are prayers, addressed to God, but in this one, the psalmist speaks directly to us, assuming the role of a spiritual director. The tone is authoritative yet intimate; this is our parent-in-God speaking

> Come, my children, and listen to me,
> and I will teach you the fear of YHWH. (v. 12)

The fear of YHWH—that is a positive experience for the biblical writers. Fear of YHWH is always commendable, though never easy. It means putting all your trust and hope in God, no matter what.

The tone of this psalm—affectionate yet authoritative—sounds to me for all the world like the Apostle Paul, and especially Paul as he writes to one of his favorite churches, the beloved congregation in Philippi. Paul's goal for these his children in God, who bring him so much joy, is that they too might have joy, the unshakable "joy of faith" (Phil. 1:25), and that they might live free from all fear (cf. Phil. 1:28), even in the face of much adversity. The psalmist has exactly the same goal for us: that living in a world of trouble, among threats and adversaries many and real, we might fear nothing—nothing, that is, except God.

It seems like an impossible dream, doesn't it, that anyone who doesn't live in a bubble of oblivion could live free from all fear, live continually in the mode of praise: "his praise shall ever be in my mouth"? You have to wonder, don't you: have these guys been listening to the news? Do they know about global warming and the dawning recognition that the whole human species faces a highly uncertain future? Do they listen to their parishioners? Have they sat with the young man who is right now gravely ill with melanoma, and his 29-year-old wife, who will give birth to their first child in just a few more weeks? Those are at the top of my own list of fears and anxieties as I write. Each of us has our own list (metaphorically speaking) that we bring into our prayers and into church—and if we recited them all aloud on any given occasion, no matter how joyful, we would in a few moments fill the sanctuary with plenty of empirical evidence that challenges the psalmist's calm assurance:

> . . . There is nothing lacking for those who fear
> [God].
> Lions may be without, and hunger,
> but those who seek YHWH will not lack all
> that is good. (vv. 10-11)

Unless you dismiss it as sheer foolishness, an assurance like that pushes to the fore what is probably the toughest question of the spiritual life, a question that never really goes away for any of us: Is true faith, genuine praise possible—possible for those whose eyes and minds are fully open to all the trouble in this world, the trouble that haunts the lives of even the most fortunate of us? Again, in what is surely one of the most appealing metaphors of the whole Bible, the psalmist says,

> Taste and see that YHWH is good;
> fortunate the person who takes refuge in [God].
> (v. 9)

"Taste and see that YHWH is good"—is there any other line of Scripture that appeals so directly to our felt experience of God in the world—and especially to the felt experience of Christians as we approach the altar: "Taste and see. . . ." Yet the truth question must be posed: Is it possible to taste—really taste life, and still come to the conclusion that "YHWH is good," and further, that "those who seek YHWH will not lack all that is good"?

The psalms are poems, and like all poems, they capture a moment, a shimmering insight, and we who read and pray them have to set that moment in the larger context of a life-situation, in order to make sense of it. That is why I turn to the Apostle Paul to understand our psalm. His life offers that context, because like the psalmist, he has faith—no, more: he has a *joy* in faith that is unshaken by much trouble. The Apostle, who spent almost all his Christian life deep in trouble, could easily have penned the psalmist's words, and almost certainly he prayed them:

> This wretch cried out, and YHWH heard,
> and from all his troubles he saved him. (v. 7)

And again:

> I sought YHWH and he answered me,
> and from all my terrors he delivered me. (v. 5)

There is not in the whole letter to the Philippians the slightest hint of fear, although Paul is writing "in chains" (Phil. 1:7, 13, 14). In this most upbeat of all Paul's letters, his attention (like the psalmist's) is wholly riveted on the goodness of God, and that is where he would have our attention as well: "Whatever is true, whatever is honorable, whatever is righteous, whatever is noble, whatever is pleasing, whatever is commendable, if there is any excellence and anything worthy of praise, these you must dwell upon ... and the God of peace will be with you" (Phil. 4:8–9).

The key insight that Paul and the psalmist would impart is this: on the day of trouble, the day that is against us—that is when we most need to rivet our attention on the goodness of God. Further, and paradoxically, the day of trouble may be the very time when we are most able to taste the goodness of God—because, as the Bible affirms over and over in both Testaments, that is the time when the Holy One of Israel is in fact closest to us:

> YHWH is close to the broken-hearted,
> and the crushed in spirit he saves. (v. 19)

So that is why the psalmist can say with such certainty that "those who seek YHWH will not lack all that is good," for what they do not lack, even in the face of terrible loss—what they have and cannot lose, is God.

> Taste and see that YHWH is good.
> Happy are those who take refuge in [God].

A better translation of that second line: "Privileged— *'ashrei,* privileged are those who take refuge in [God]." These, the broken-hearted who shelter in God because, with the deep wisdom of the sufferer, they know they have no place else to go—contrary to all ordinary sense, they discover that their situation is indeed a "privileged" one, for what sustains them in that dark sheltered place is nothing, nothing but the total, palpable goodness of God, so close to them they can taste it with their tears.

> I will bless YHWH at all times;
> his praise shall ever be in my mouth.

Something is created in that dark place where the broken-hearted find shelter, something that Paul calls, in a luminous phrase, "the fellowship [*koinonia*] of Christ's sufferings" (Phil. 3:10). Paul is speaking of a mystery, and he doesn't try to explain what he means. "The fellowship of Christ's sufferings"—this is probably the deepest of all the mysteries that God reveals to us in this life. And all of us, I dare say, know something of that fellowship. We know it, in part, from our own personal experiences of tasting God's goodness on the day that is against us. Yet much of what we know about the fellowship of Christ's sufferings we learn from witnesses, who enable us to trust in its reality. Some crucial witnesses have gone long before us: Paul and the psalmist chief among them, and then the saints, confessors, and martyrs of the church. But others are with us now on the journey, witnessing to us by their persistent faith on the day that is against them. I don't mean that they are consciously offering a witness. Often these are the folks who ask for our prayers and thank us for coming to visit. But we know it is *their* prayers, their adamant sheltering in God, that strengthens us, inspires us, enables us to taste God's goodness in the midst of experience that, to the undiscerning palate, would be entirely bitter.

"The fellowship of Christ's sufferings"—I glimpsed it in recent weeks as the young man suffering from melanoma enabled his grandmother, a woman who had lived 80-plus years without any active faith, to get past her rage at the cancer that was consuming her own body. Gently he guided her into the church and introduced her to the sacrament—"Taste and see that YHWH is good"—so she might die without fear. And she did—miraculously, to those who know her best. She died knowing herself to be the beloved child of God. Those who suffer in God are probably the best teachers in the church. With their incomparable wisdom, they initiate others into that mystical fellowship in which trouble is transformed—not denied, or eliminated, much as we would wish it so—but transformed, forever changed. In the *koinonia* of Christ's sufferings, trouble is transubstantiated into deeper participation in God's incarnate life in this, our aching world.

Those blessed teachers, those witnesses are with us each time we come to the altar. We carry them with us in our prayers, and they carry us on the strength of their faith, deeper into the life of the God who is known beyond all doubt to be "close to the broken-hearted," who

> . . . redeems the life of his servants,
> so that all who take refuge in him will never be
> condemned. (v. 23)

We might hear the invitation of this wise and blessed teacher each time we draw near the altar, with the broken-hearted as our guides to it and our companions at it—inviting us to come time and again, on the day that is for us and on the day that is against us, and always to "Taste, and see that YHWH is good."

Notes

1. YHWH is a transliteration of the Hebrew name of God, traditionally too sacred to be pronounced. In the Book of Common Prayer translation of the psalms, it is rendered "LORD." All translations here are my own, following the Hebrew numbering of the verses, which in the psalms often differs slightly from the English numbering (plus one).

2. From "Ali, the Companion of Muhammad." Cf. Sachiko Murata and William Chittick, *The Vision of Islam* (New York: Paragon House, 1994), 30. The Arabic word *subr* may mean "have patience" or "endure."

Emmaus: Christ Between

Rowan Williams

WALKING TOGETHER in the company of Christ is what the Church is all about. But as we all know—especially those in positions of leadership—it is appallingly difficult. And the question is how we relate to each other in the Church in such a way that we see Christ between us.

I offer this reflection in tribute to a dear friend and disciple who has struggled with this at a costly time in the Anglican Church—and as a prayer that we shall all find the path on which we can together listen to the risen Jesus.

First the sun, then the shadow,
so that I screw my eyes to see
my friend's face, and its lines seem
different, and the voice shakes in the hot air.
Out of the rising white dust, feet
tread a shape, and, out of step,
another flat sound, stamped between voice
and ears, dancing in the gaps, and dodging
where words and feet do not fall.

When our eyes meet, I see bewilderment
(like mine); we cannot learn
the rhythm we are asked to walk,
and what we hear is not each other.
Between us is filled up, the silence
is filled up, lines of our hands
and faces pushed into shape
by the solid stranger, and the static
breaks up our waves like dropped stones.

So it is necessary to carry him with us,
cupped between hands and profiles,
so that the table is filled up, and as
the food is set and the first wine splashes,
a solid thumb and finger tear the thunderous
grey bread. Now it is cold, even indoors,
and the light falls sharply on our bones;
the rain breathes out hard, dust blackens,
and our released voices shine with water.

God's Life with Us:
Reconciling the Irreconcilable

Kathryn Tanner

Reconciliation is more than a human task. It is our willing participation in what God has already done. Paul makes it very clear that, in and through the incarnation, death and resurrection of Christ, God was reconciling the world to God's self and by extension the world and all persons in it to one another.

FRANK T. GRISWOLD

THE PRESIDING BISHOP in this Pauline meditation on reconciliation uncovers the root of our efforts as Christians to be together with one another in our differences through love. At the heart of those efforts is God's own way of being for us. We have been shown the way of God and have been graced to participate in it through Jesus Christ our Lord, in the power of his Spirit. That way of God ever precedes us, as something that we can count on in the midst of all our failings, something to which we can always pin our otherwise faltering hopes. Swept up into the life of God by what has been accomplished for us in Christ, we are to be caught up in, and so demonstrate in our own lives, the shape of God's own dealings with us.

Those dealings proclaim, from the beginning when God creates the world to the end when God saves it, the unheard-of good news of reconciliation. At odds with one another, apparent incompatibles are to be brought together in the all-spanning love of the triune God. And, in virtue of being so united in love, these differences from one another are not to be destroyed but perfected in all their irreducible particularity.

It is the very greatest difference of all—between the infinite majesty of God's eternal holiness and the finite world of sin and death—that God bridges through the love that constitutes God's own intra-Trinitarian life, directed outward for the good of creatures. The depth of God's gracious love for a dying and depraved world may become increasingly clear as the Christian story of creation and salvation unfolds and finally comes to its climax in the death and resurrection of Christ. But it is the same God of our Lord Jesus Christ who acts in the same way, with the same intent, from the beginning of the story to the end. God wishes to perfect the goodness of what is different from God—the whole created, non-divine world—in its very difference from God, through the most intimate possible relationship with it. In virtue of that very closeness of relationship, the supreme goodness of God's life is to become our own, while we yet remain who and what we are—the finite, fallible creatures, in and of ourselves, of a God who is in those respects so very different from us.

Creation, the beginning of the story of God's dealings with us, is itself then a story of reconciliation. Differences between God and the world that seem irreconcilable are bridged by God's involvement with the world as its creator, an involvement that respects those differences rather than dissolving them. Underlying the message that Christians perhaps take for granted in its obviousness and simplicity—God brings the world to be and upholds it in existence—is a problem to be resolved, a kind of ontological antagonism, between apparently opposed kinds of things, requiring reconciliation. To the Greco-Roman world, in which Christian religious reflection developed, and perhaps to the common sense of every day and age, it is hard to imagine what things so different from one another could possibly have to do with another. How can God, perfect in all respects, be involved with the world as we know it, a world rife with decay, corruption, failure, and conflict?

If God and the world are this different from one another, God, one might think, must sit at a remove from the world. Divine principles of a lesser perfection are the only ones able to come into direct contact with it. Those lesser divine principles establish a protective buffer zone between the highest divinity and a world so unlike it.

The religious problem here simply takes its rise from a more general, commonsensical principle. Like mixes with like; and therefore the different must take their leave of one another. Light with light, darkness with darkness; light and darkness to be separated since their conjunction can come about only at their mutual peril. Brought together they can only corrupt or dissipate one another.

Following this general idea, Greco-Romans assume that incompatibles can be reconciled with one another only if they are really more like one another than they first appear. Perhaps God isn't all that different from the world as we know it. Maybe God—or, we should now say the gods and goddesses of the Greco-Roman pantheon—are very much like those rather sorry, conflict-riddled aspects of the world for which they take responsibility. The god involved with battles between men, Ares, is himself belligerent, a warrior in clashes among the gods themselves; and so on. Or, perhaps the world, at least in certain respects, is more like God than we give it credit for. God remains supremely perfect but there are immortal, unchangeable sides to the world existing above the fray of its division and contest—for example, mathematical truths, eternal souls—which are like God and which therefore God has something to do with.

Christians, however, maintain that the world in all its respects is different from God. The world in its entirety is finite and therefore changeable and prone to corruption and conflict—and God is none of those things. But God is nonetheless directly concerned with this world in an all-embracing love for what is different from God. God brings that world to be, in delight for what is other than God, in an effort to see the good of God's own life replicated as far as possible in resplendent gifts to something genuinely other. And God upholds that world which is not God, remains faithful to it, despite its falling away from the good that God intends for it, despite its awful actual descent into all the possibilities for failure in finitude, in a steadfast unwavering love for the world. God continues to be near, at our beck and call. Turning to the proffered goods of God's own life would dissipate the harms we have brought upon ourselves but not the essential difference between God and creatures. The value and integrity of creatures are to be respected in the transformations to be expected from intimacy with the divine life.

God's concern as creator for the world as we know it is, in short, both comprehensive and direct. Nothing is exempt because of its dissimilarity from God. God's love is to be felt in both good times and bad, in conflict and in peace, in the horrors of life and at its heights—indeed, especially at those times of the greatest terror and woe since we are most in need then of God's continuing beneficent grace. And when God comes to us he is himself the gift giver, our helper and savior without substitute, because the Greco-Roman principle of like-with-like has been overthrown. God's nature is not compromised or corrupted by coming into close contact with things of an opposed nature—the way, say, fire needs to be kept from corruption, from the loss of its own nature, through contact by water. Nor, conversely, need divinity compromise the created natures of things different from itself when brought into intimate relation with them—the way fire compromises the nature of water—dissipating it into the air—by heating it. God meets us in love, to better us, as the beings we are, in a continuing expression of gracious regard for the non-divine, specifically as such.

Because we fail to avail ourselves of the good that God ceaselessly offers to us in the nearness of his love as creator, God chooses, as savior of the world, to take that very humanity suffering under the weight of sin to himself in Christ. Reconciling the incompatibles of divinity and created humanity in a veritable unity of love this time, God establishes a relationship of unsurpassable closeness with Christ's own humanity, a relationship of virtual identification. God is now to be identified with this human being Jesus; this human being Jesus is God. Come to save us in the very midst of our misery and sin, this God, again, is no inferior or subordinate deity but very God, the one and only highest God. And in being so identified, neither the divinity of God nor the humanity of Jesus, we are taught, is compromised. Instead, God remains God to raise up the humanity of Christ, perfected and healed. In the resurrected life of the crucified one we see the goods of God's own life, such as immortality, transferred to someone who nevertheless remains fully human as we are.

It is this closing of the gap between humanity and divinity in Christ that bridges the scandalous, and in that sense greater divide between God and a sinful world. We are in touch with God in the highest and with neither a demi-god nor a super-man when we are in touch with Christ. And yet we are so with the greatest possible physical intimacy. Here is very God walking upon the earth as a man so that we might grab the hem of his garments, receive his spit on our faces, and feel his hands upon our skin to heal. After his death, in a way that overcomes all temporal and spatial absences on earth, we are blessed in the power of his Spirit to feed upon his very flesh and blood to our eternal nourishment in Eucharistic fellowship.

We do so, not as those favored by God because of our holiness and right living, but as suffering sinners in desperate need of reconciliation with God in all his goodness, if we are to live anew. Christ comes in order to overcome the divide between God and world that sin and its awful consequences for human life open up. And therefore he comes not for the righteous and the already well off, but for sinners and sufferers, for all those who seem cut off and excluded from God's righteousness and beneficent love.

It is as we are united with the reconciling love that is Christ's own life through the power of his Spirit that we are to be renewed and refreshed, brought to our completion as the creatures we are, sin and its consequences in destruction and hurt made to end. United to Christ as the creatures we are, we are yet enabled to enjoy the goods of God's own life as our own. Because we are one with God in Christ, the goods proper to God are now as much our own as God's.

Not even the antagonism of a sinful world can break the hold that God in his mercy has on the world in Christ. Christ goes to his death, rejected by the sinners he comes to serve, but that very death, united now with the power of God in Christ's own life, provides the means for its overcoming. Suffering and decay, made Christ's own, are overthrown, so that sinfulness loses its sting.

Armed with the pacific knowledge of this reconciling work of God in Christ, to which we are enjoined by his Spirit, let awareness of our manifest failings not dissuade us from the hope that we may be reconciled in Christ to one another. The antagonisms bred of our differences may even now be overwhelmed by the love God has for us in Christ, the good that comes of such differences respected, their hostilities winnowed away.

A Fresh Look at the Synod of Whitby: A Mark of Unity and Reconciliation

Esther de Waal

I T WAS, OF COURSE, through St. Benedict that we first met, in the days when I organized weeks of Benedictine experience in the Diocese of Chicago and Frank Griswold was bishop. I've always been aware of the monastic undergirding of all that Frank does and says, and in particular what he says about listening with the heart. so to write about an apparent clash of monastic cultures and reveal the deeper concern for unity and reconciliation seems an appropriate way in which to celebrate the friendship of someone whose life has been such a demonstration of these values.

The story of the Synod of Whitby has been told and retold many times. In recent years, encouraged by the widespread enthusiasm for all things Celtic, it has been presented as a conflict between the Roman and the Celtic, in which a futile last stand was made by the Celtic church against the power of centralizing Rome. Thus it is seen as cataclysmic, a disastrous confrontation, after which all those good things that Celtic Christianity stood for were driven underground—until once again they are being recovered and, in many instances, relived today.

This interpretation was very clearly established in 1987 by Shirley Toulson in her aptly titled *The Celtic Alternative: A Reminder of the Christianity We Lost.* "When matters came to a head at Whitby," she wrote, "and the Celtic church ceased to exist, we lost a form of individual Christianity which through its druidic roots, was truly linked to the perennial philosophy of humanity...."[1] Since then that theme has been repeated, not least by Philip Newell, who is quite categorical: "Essentially the conflict was between two radically different ways of seeing." He tells us that the Celtic mission argued from the authority of John, the beloved disciple, leaning against Christ at the Last Supper and listening for the heartbeat of God, while the Roman mission appealed to the authority of Peter, the rock on which Christ had promised to build his church. He sees the outcome as a tragedy, a momentous decision that was to alter the complexion of Christianity, not only in Britain but in much of the Western world.[2] Time and again it is described in terms of a clash in which "the Roman Church stands for an ecclesiastical empire that needed conformity to function properly."[3]

The Synod is thus generally presented in adversarial terms as an encounter between opposing forces. Sadly, this has been repeatedly used by both Anglicans and Roman Catholics to defend their positions against one another.[4] Today we are watching a further development as Whitby is being used within denominations in an attempt to recover values and practices that are claimed to be those of the Celtic church, such as being non-hierarchical, having a creation-centered spirituality, emphasizing the role of the feminine, living with a sense of the presence of God in daily life. The list could easily be continued.[5] To sustain this the *Carmina Gadelica*, a nineteenth-century compilation based on oral tradition in the Outer Hebrides, is frequently taken as evidence of a timeless Celtic spirituality with total disregard of awareness of historical development. Nor is it always commonly remembered that we owe the image of the wild goose as the Holy Spirit to George McLeod and the phrase "a thin place," to Evelyn Underhill.[6]

When I set myself the task of questioning the popular view of the Synod of Whitby I did so for a number of reasons, not least the debt that I myself owe to Celtic spirituality.[7] But I also believe that here we have a story that is both more fascinating and more important than its popular misrepresentation. What really happened in 664 at Whitby? The fact is that it was no more than a local council, common enough at the time, called by a politically motivated king for immediate practical reasons. R. W. Southern, arguably the greatest medieval ecclesiastical historian of the twentieth century, reminds us that any writing about the church must never be separated from secular history. It is vitally important "to appreciate the forces which confined and directed the development of the church."[8] A recent book by Rowan Williams carries the subtitle "The Quest for the Historical Church."[9] Trained as a historian, I believe that it has become more urgent than ever before to look to the past and to learn from it, above all trying to handle evidence responsibly and put personalities and events into their proper context.

Missionary Monasticism

It was by way of monasticism, whether Celtic or Roman, that Christianity first reached the shores of Britain. Without making this the essential starting point, any appreciation of the seventh century is impossible. For the inhabitants of the British Isles at this period, whether Saxon or Celtic, the monastery was the primary focus for their religion. It brought into their lives not only worship, but pastoral care, and teaching, and not least beauty.[10] The figures of authority in the church tended to be abbots, many of whom reluctantly accepted the office of bishop, while remaining monastic at heart, and whenever possible returning to end their days in a monastery.

Influenced by the local milieu and not least by the secular patrons who knew how to combine piety with shrewd politics, these monastic communities did not practice separation from the world; rather they were actively engaged in it at all levels. They saw their main work as that of evangelization. The Christian message was spread through a network of monastic centers, whether monks and nuns, and occasionally double communities. There was a fine balance between the life of prayer and pastoral and missionary activity. No one doubted the inestimable power of prayer, and when it came to prayer the women were more than the equals of the men. Convents, which were generally larger than male monasteries since many well-to-do families placed their daughters there, became veritable powerhouses of prayer.

Paganism was still rife and the monks and nuns were faced by both an indigenous pagan people and by the massive invasions of heathen tribes after the Romans left Britain. Their most urgent concern was therefore conversion: the salvation of the souls of a people who felt themselves surrounded by the spirit world and for whom fear was never far away. This was no romantic landscape. It was an unsafe world inhabited by dark forces that had to be placated. Dealing with a largely illiterate population, they found that the oral and the visual played an important role, and Christian shrines and saints brought holy places and holy people into a largely untamed spiritual landscape. Christianity spread at ground level, radiating out from scattered centers in what Peter Brown describes as a gradual process, "through intermittent, highly charged contact with the sacred; through high moments of festival, through pilgrimage to high places, through memorable supernatural duels between Christian holy persons and their visible and invisible enemies—sorcerers, demons, fire and the bleak hostility of the northern weather."[11]

Cross and Resurrection

Whether the mission was Celtic or Roman, the cross was central. Celtic Christianity was never "creation-centered." It was certainly creation-filled. Celtic writing brings us magnificent literary expressions of their love of the earth and of nature, but then all monasticism is profoundly incarnational, and in particular the Benedictine tradition. Benedict reverenced matter and the physical, paid respect to the tools of daily life and not least to husbandry and the responsible cultivation of the soil. But for both, the paschal mystery was the heart of their life. The portrayal of the crucifixion, whether in Northumbria or Ireland, was however very different from that of the early Middle Ages. Death and resurrection were seen as two aspects of one single event, and what they emphasized was the transition from darkness and death to light and new life. As a result (and this would have seemed natural in a society in which warrior kings were still a powerful presence), the suffering Christ was also the heroic triumphant Christ rescuing his people and setting them free.[12]

Christ's death was linked to his resurrection; the victorious Christ led to the new life of Easter.

Easter was the pivotal moment of the year on which everything else depended. St. Patrick on the hill of Slane had lit the fire of the Easter vigil and the courtiers of the heathen king watching from the hill of Tara had predicted that once lit it would never be put out. At the Easter vigil, baptism (still at this time adult baptism) took place with all its powerful symbolism of entering into the waters, into the tomb of death, and emerging to renounce Satan and turning to face Christ. It is a reminder that "the theology of the early Christians was the result of symbols deeply lived."[13]

Celebration of Easter made Christian believers aware of their unity with the church in other times and places. It also brought them into the ebb and flow of creation, for as Bede observed in the letter to Nectan, the whole universe was involved:

> We are commanded to keep the full moon of
> the paschal month after the vernal equinox, the
> object being that the sun should first make the
> day longer than the night and then the moon
> can show to the world her full orb of light be-
> cause the "Sun of righteousness with healing

in his wings" (Mat 4.2), that is, the Lord Jesus, overcame all the darkness of death by the triumph of his resurrection.[14]

Since a festival in spring was already familiar, it is hardly surprising to learn that the name given to this new feast should come, as Bede tells us in his book on natural science, from the goddess Eostre. "By that name they now called the time of pascha, customary observance giving its name to a new solemnity."[15]

The Calendar

The calendric calculation, however, was extremely intricate, a technical issue that concerned conflicting systems of computation. Theological and doctrinal matters were not at stake: it was purely a practical matter. Nor was there was anything particularly "Celtic" about it; the Council of Arles had tackled it in 314, the Council of Toledo in 633. The Irish were using a lunar system that had reached them from Rome, made on a ninety-five-year cycle and much less accurate than those that replaced them in 525 based on a lunar cycle of 532 years. The variant reading could mean a difference of celebration of anything from one to four weeks apart, so that the two Easter dates might sometimes be wildly disparate. The year 664 was a case in point. In the Northumbrian court Bede tells us that "Easter was kept twice in the same year, so that when the king had ended Lent and was keeping Easter, the queen and her attendants were still fasting and keeping Palm Sunday." Life in a royal court divided in this way must have been difficult, not to say embarrassing, since not only did Easter bring a return to full meals but also a normal sex life after the Lenten abstinence.[16]

Rome

Some thirty years before Whitby the southern Irish had decided to settle the date and sent delegates to Rome, "the chief of cities." They arrived at Eastertide in 631 "as children to their mother," staying in one of the pilgrim hostels that clustered right up to the very walls of the great basilica. "And they were in one lodging in the church of St. Peter with a Greek, a Hebrew, a Scythian and an Egyptian at the same time at Easter." Being together with others from many different nations gave them a shared experience of the universality of the church, and they returned to Ireland convinced of the rightness of the Roman Easter.[17] After this the southern Irish kept the Roman dating, and Cummian, a learned man who had studied the subject, wrote to his fellow-Irishman Columba telling him that he and his proud sons were now out of touch with the rest of the world, and his community "no more than a pimple on the chin of the earth."

The Rome of this period was the city of Peter and Paul, not yet the city of the papal monarchy. The pilgrims who went there (and there was a widespread longing to make a pilgrimage to Rome) visited the shrines and basilicas in and around the city, through what was known as the stational system.[18] Saints were a real presence—the expression still found in Africa, "the living dead," is a reminder of how immediate the sense of connectedness to the deceased may be.

To experience the appropriate liturgy successively at

each of the shrines was an expression of diversity in unity that strengthened the feeling: a sense of connectedness to other members of the church, whether in heaven or on earth. It is therefore hardly surprising to learn of the interest of Brigit in the Roman liturgy—and it seems useful to remember this aspect of her life. The story is found in an early text, possibly dating back to about 650. A holy man when visiting the house found her at prayer with hands outstretched to heaven, "and she did not see or hear anything else" even though there was a great deal of noise since the calves had just then been rushed to the cows. When he asked her why she did not run when there was all the shouting, she replied that she had heard nothing. "I hear masses in Rome at the tombs of Ss. Peter and Paul and it is my earnest wish that the order of the mass and of the universal rule he brought to me." She immediately sent experts to Rome to bring back the latest liturgical development, and when she discerned that there had been further changes she asked them to return, "and they went and brought it back as they had found it."[19]

The Celtic Church?

At this point, therefore, we are bound to ask if there was ever any such thing as the "Celtic church." In spite of certain social and cultural divergences within the Celtic lands themselves—and after all they ranged from Brittany and Cornwall to Scotland—they were all shaped by the one thing they had in common, their isolation from the mainstream European tradition. "They lagged far behind," as Nora Chadwick put it, retaining primitive Christian institutions long after these had been subjected to gradual changes elsewhere. These differences however were not fundamental and in no sense were they doctrinal.[20] In spite of this distant geographical location they themselves never felt that they were ideologically apart from the rest of Christendom. Travel whether by land or sea, though it might often be difficult and dangerous, did not prevent the constant interplay of people and ideas. The Irish Columbanus described his fellow Christians to Pope Boniface as living "at the edge of the world," but, he continued, they knew themselves to be "pupils of Saints Peter and Paul and of all the disciples who were inspired by the Holy Spirit . . . and we accepted nothing beyond the teaching of the Gospels and the Apostles. . . . Our possession of the catholic faith is unshaken, we hold it just as it was first handed to us by you, the successors of the holy apostles."[21]

This was still the church of the first millennium. Ought we not to remember the way in which it was made up of numerous regional variations stretching like so many beads on a string from Iona across Europe and to the Middle East? Until the schism of East and West in 1054 it brought far-flung places together into what Peter Brown has so nicely called a Christian global village.[22] How then does the "Celtic church" (and its demise) fit into this picture?

Whitby

The Synod of Whitby was simply a local council called by King Oswy, who wanted to gather the leading clerics and monastics of his kingdom in order to deal with a number of immediate problems, not least the divisions within his own family. He was in trouble with his rebellious and ambitious son Aldfrith, who was ruling a part of Northumbria as sub-king and was a close ally of the pro-Saxon cleric Wilfred and thus in opposition to his father. His wife Eanflaed came from Kent and had received her Christian faith from Canterbury, as did her retinue, while his own faith and that of many others at the court came from Iona. This as we saw earlier might mean a court split between those keeping Lent and those celebrating Easter.

The favorable outcome of the debate—and there can be little doubt that the king had made up his mind from the start—enabled Oswy to unite his court, to be in step with his wife, and to deal with a potentially dangerous son. In addition it would be useful to have the support of the see of Canterbury in his power struggles with the king of Mercia. When the Saxon Wilfred finished speaking, the king asked "with a smile, that famous question: 'Tell me which is the greater in the Kingdom of Heaven, Columba or the Apostle Peter?'" The response gave the king what he wanted.

So can it be right to call it a humiliation, a momentous defeat for the Celtic side? Can it be seen as a confrontation that ended in bitter recrimination? When Colman returned to Iona with thirty or so English monks who wished to follow the way of Columba, in addition to the Irish monks he still retained the affection and respect of the king and took with him some of the relics of Aidan. Both Hilda and Cuthbert were now amongst those who accepted the new dating. Oswy found no difficulty in appointing one of Aidan's disciples as abbot of Lindisfarne. Bede, even though he took a definitely partisan view, wrote warmly of the Irish, "The sole concern of these teachers was to serve God and not the world. . ." The fraternal friendship and fruitful collaboration between the Irish and Northumbrian Christianity continued to determine church life for the next hundred years. In many things, not least in the arts, Saxon monasteries owed a huge debt to the Irish, "at all times receiving them warmly as elder brothers and sisters in Christ and borrowing generously from these generous elders," in the charming words of Thomas Cahill.[23]

Lindisfarne

I want to conclude by turning to visual rather than written evidence. The purpose of the Lindisfarne Gospels, finished about thirty years after Whitby, was to portray Cuthbert as "the great Reconciler." The work of Northumbrian monks, it brought together many traditions, Irish, English, Roman, and Coptic, blending them into one glorious and harmonious whole. It has been called by a modern calligrapher a visual statement of the unification of the various streams of Christian orthodoxy lived by the church in Northumbria at that time, at once both distinctly local and universal. "This is not a Celtic, Columban or Irish book as opposed to a Roman one, but in fact one that is consciously stating a unified position beyond them."[24] The great authority on this book speaks of its "combined ethnicity, and sees it bringing together elements as diversified as Byzantine and Coptic, Pictish and Frankish, all components of the universal church. We are brought back again to the celebration of unity and diversity![25]

Final Reflections

What is all this saying? Where does this leave us? Each reader must dialogue with this essay in their own way. The stories I have told here speak of unity and diversity, and of how differences and divergencies can be enriching. Conflicts are inevitable, so we may as well learn how to handle them, as in seventh-century Northumbria, so that friendship and cooperation grow from them. I would hope, in the context of a new look at Whitby, that the time has come to bury any idea of "the Celtic church" and instead to resurrect the role of "the church of the first millennium."

I think that a study such as this carries the warning that the history of the church when divorced from secular history can go wrong, and that spirituality when divorced from history can go very wrong indeed. Every generation rereads and rewrites the past. The danger is that we set out to find what we are looking for. Perhaps the last word should lie with St. Gregory the Great—the man who sent Augustine to England, the correspondent of Columbanus, the pope who retained the heart and vision of the monk. He points us to the image of the watchman, the one who takes "a wide survey and prays for the grace to see life whole and power to speak effectively of it."[26]

Notes

1. Shirley Toulson, *The Celtic Alternative: A Reminder of the Christianity We Lost* (London: Rider, 1987), 9.

2. J. Philip Newell, *Listening for the Heartbeat of God: A Celtic Spirituality* (New York: Paulist, 1997), and *The Book of Creation: The Practice of Celtic Spirituality* (Norwich: Canterbury Press, 1999).

There is no time here to go into the other conflict about which he writes extensively—Pelagius (good) versus Augustine (bad).

3. The phrase is taken from Brendan Lehane, *Early Celtic Christianity* (London: Constable, 1994), 191, but it could be replicated many times over.

4. There is a valuable article on this subject by Arthur G. Holder, "Whitby and All That: The Search for Anglican Origins," *Anglican Theological Review* 85, no. 2, 231–52.

5. A far more interesting and useful topic might be to consider to what extent much of this is common to any primal peoples throughout the world—the aborigines of Australia, the Indians of North America, traditional African culture, peoples close to the earth who know about kin and kinship, and for whom the oral tradition remains important.

6. See *The Collected Papers of Evelyn Underhill* (London: Longmans, Green and Co., 1946), 196, in a lecture on Education and the Spirit of Worship, given in 1937. I owe this to my brother-in-law the Rev. Dr. C. Armstrong, who refers to it in his biography of Evelyn Underhill, now sadly out of print.

7. Above all it has taught me much about the relationship between prayer and the imagination. *The Celtic Way of Prayer: The Recovery of the Religious Imagination*, really says it all (the title of a book published in 1997).

8. *Western Society and the Church in the Middle Ages* (London: Penguin, 1970), 15–16.

9. *Why Study the Past? The Quest for the Historical Church.* Sarum Theological College Lectures (London: Darton, Longman & Todd, 2005).

10. "The monasterium, whether cathedral, parish church or other institution, provides the still and stable centre, the pool of prayer, psalmody and spirituality from which all can drink and refresh themselves." Ian Bradley has some interesting things to say about monastic centers in *Colonies of Heaven: Celtic Models for Today's Church* (London: Darton, Longman & Todd, 2000).

11. Peter Brown, *The Rise of Western Christendom: Triumph and Diversity 200–1000* (Malden, Mass.: Blackwell, 1996), 227.

12. There is a great deal written about Celtic crosses. Less well known is the Saxon material. See Barbara C. Raw, *Anglo-Saxon Crucifixion: Iconograph and the Art of the Monastic Revival* (Cambridge: Cambridge University Press, 1990).

13. Thomas M. Finn says this in his *Early Baptism and the Catechumenate,* vol. 6 (Minneapolis: Liturgical Press, 1992), 5.

14. *High King of Heaven: Aspects of Early English Spirituality* (London: Mowbray, 1999), 17, 19 note 11.

15. Ibid.

16. Thomas Owen Clancy and Gilbert Markus, *Iona: The Earliest Poetry of a Celtic Monastery* (Edinburgh: Edinburgh University Press, 1995), 9, 14, and Benedicta Ward, op. cit., 19–20.

17. Eamonn O. Carragain, *The City of Rome and the World of Bede,* Jarrow Lecture 1994.

18. Peter Brown, op. cit., 223.

19. Eamonn O. Carragain, op. cit. The cult of the saints was widespread throughout Latin Christendom; see Peter Brown, *The Cult of the Saints* (Chicago: University of Chicago Press, 1981).

20. Nora K. Chadwick, *Early Brittany* (Cardiff: University of Wales Press, 1969), 270.

21. Peter Brown, op. cit., 232. He also gives us the phrase "regionalized micro-Christendom."

22. See the fascinating chapter "Columba and Columbanus," in Douglas Dales's *Light to the Isles: Missionary Theology in Celtic and Anglo Saxon Britain* (Cambridge: Lutterworth Press, 1997), an important study.

23. *How the Irish Saved Civilization* (New York: Doubleday, 1995), 202.

24. Ewan Clayton, *Embracing Change: Spirituality and the Lindisfarne Gospels* (2003).

25. Michelle Brown is the leading expert on the Lindisfarne Gospels. See *In the Beginning Was the Word: Books and Faith in the Age of Bede,* Jarrow Lecture 2000. Arthur Holder also makes the same point speaking of "a synthesis of multiple traditions" in his article, p. 250.

26. 25 Homilies of Pope Gregory the Great on the Book of Ezekiel, Book 1, 11, 4–6.

Trinitarian Life: The Source of Reconciliation

Mark McIntosh

W HAT DOES JESUS WANT to bestow upon creation? In Jesus' intimacy with his companions
before Calvary, the Gospel of John portrays him as
drawing others into his own relationship with the One
he calls Father: "I do not call you servants any longer,
because the servant does not know what the master
is doing; but I have called you friends, because I have
made known to you everything that I have heard from
my Father" (John 15:15). Jesus brings his followers into
a new state of being, friendship, a state of being one
with another in love and freedom, a state of reconciliation. And this state, in John's view, is only possible for
humanity as it is led by Jesus into an ever-deepening
participation in that inexhaustible sharing of life which
is the Trinity: "I have called you friends, because I have
made known to you everything that I have heard from
my Father." The Presiding Bishop has often led his
hearers into these scenes from the Farewell Discourses
in John, opening for us and sharing with us something
of that new relationship of friendship with God which
has been the wellspring of Bishop Frank's own ministry.

In this essay, I want to express my thanks for what God has been doing through the ministry of the Primate by offering a way of thinking about the Trinity that may be helpful to souls. My basic point is simply this: God the blessed Trinity reconciles and overcomes all sinful divisions in the universe by bringing the creatures within the peaceful communion of trinitarian life ("I have called you friends"); what we experience as reconciliation is nothing less than the conversion of our divisions towards the difference-in-unity of the Persons of the Trinity. Intelligent creatures have the capacity to be drawn into deeper awareness of this creating and reconciling, this laboring of the Trinity; by prayerful attunement with it, they may become more willing and effective ministers of reconciliation themselves. There is no dimension of creaturely existence—whether personal, ecclesial, global, or cosmic—where this laboring of the Trinity is absent or its power to bring about new and reconciled life is without witness, the first and last and ever true witness always being the crucified and risen Christ himself.

While this reconciling, communion-forging life of the Trinity is, of course, the fundamental mystery of our universe and so always beyond conceptual grasp, the church lives by constantly nourishing itself and being continually converted in the presence of this mystery. Part of that process of continual conversion is what ancient Christians called *theōria* in Greek or *contemplatio* in Latin, the giving over of our whole heart and mind to the joyful and transforming gazing at this mystery of the trinitarian life. Apart from this contemplative theological conversion, the church's mind is easily captivated by urgencies and mesmerized by fears that distort its hearing and proclamation of the gospel; but as the church gives itself to this ever-deepening conversion, it is disposed to a more effective witnessing of God's work. St. Gregory of Nyssa likens this patient and prayerful nourishing of the church's mind to the experience of one drawing near to gaze upon an inexhaustible source of life:

> If anyone happened to be near the fountain which scripture says [Gen. 2:6] rose from the earth at the beginning of creation and was large enough to water the earth's surface, he would approach it marveling at the endless stream of water gushing forth and bubbling out. Never could he say that he had seen all the water. . . . In the same way, the person looking at the divine, invisible beauty will always discover it anew since he will see it as something newer and more wondrous in comparison to what he had already comprehended. He continues to wonder at God's continuous revelation; he never exhausts his desire to see more because what he awaits is always more magnificent and more divine than anything he has seen.[1]

We can never come to the end of God's wonders. Whatever good we grasp will only be exceeded by a yet greater share in God's goodness—if we will permit our hearts and minds to be overtaken by this infinite self-sharing of trinitarian life. As the church unstintingly gives itself to this true worship of God, it is the more genuine and quick-eyed in its ministry of reconciliation in the world.

Good theology can help us to gaze worshipfully and nourishingly into this mystery. In that spirit we ask: How does the Trinity come to embrace creaturely divisions within the unity-in-difference of the Divine Persons? What is this friendship that Jesus is bringing to birth? Christians believe that, having been created in the image of God the Trinity, we are created for relation, for being one with another in love and freedom, for friendship. We might describe sin as the distortion of relations, so that what was meant for joy and life is often vexing, risky, and sometimes even mortal. The result is that human relations have grown tenuous. Seldom, this side of Eden, do creaturely relations bear within themselves the secret wellspring of the trinitarian relations which are their eternal source. Insofar as human relations, meant to be the flowing source of love within the world, have grown stunted and embittered, so the divine abundance they were meant to mediate is lost to us.

For this reason John's Gospel understands Jesus' initiation of his disciples into his relation with the Father as the climax of a long and painfully ironic struggle. Throughout the Gospel, Jesus has encountered many who respond to his words and deeds with what John portrays as a characteristic human literalness, incapable of perceiving or receiving the fullness of divine abundance and self-sharing life: Nicodemus understands new birth in narrowly biological terms, the Samaritan woman hopes for living water that is merely persistently wet, Martha looks for the resurrection of her brother Lazarus only at the last day, and so on. John views all this as a particularly painful irony since the one whom the world misunderstands in so constricting a manner is the inexhaustibly abundant Word of the Father in whom and through whom all these things have come to be. Ironically, they fail to hear the full depths of the very creative Word through whom they have their own existence.

Jesus, we could say, is the incarnate presence of God's primordial meaning for each creature; he is the truth of God's deep desire for each creature in all its fullness, as it might have been and might yet, in him, become. And he is this Word of God to us precisely as he opens to us his relation to the Father. It is as though the very master idea of a playwright, by means of which she had conceived an entire play—and which was, therefore, the crucial inner truth and potential and goal of absolutely everything in the play—also came to be embodied by the playwright as a particular character within her play. When Jesus encounters others, his words and actions with them are a continual epiphany of God's eternal longing and desire for each one of them, opening up within their lives a living spring of that very same holy desire, Holy Spirit, by which they might each be drawn towards the fullness of God's original Logos or idea for them, their maturity in Christ: "While Jesus was standing [in the Temple], he cried out, 'Let anyone who is thirsty come to me, and let the one who believes in me drink. As the scripture has said, "Out of the believer's heart shall flow rivers of living water.' Now he said this about the Spirit, which believers in him were to receive" (John 7:37–39).

Jesus' encounters with others are so radiant, and sometimes bewildering, because they expose those whom he meets to God's deepest truth about themselves, and in those moments, the deep longing and desiring of their hearts is released so that the infinitely deeper longing, the relational desiring of God the Spirit, wells up within them; this overflows and carries away the small, embittered, meandering desires and fears that had for so long captivated and stunted them. John draws us into a paradigm case of this liberating flowing forth of truth in the Farewell Discourses—where, not coincidentally, Jesus speaks both of the disciples' abiding in his love (keeping his "word," that is, God's intention and meaning) and of the Spirit outpouring the realization and meaning of that word via their relations with each other. Then the Holy Spirit will "teach you everything, and remind you of all that I have said to you" (John 14:26) and this will mean being caught up in the same love and delight that animate Jesus in his relation with the Father, knowing himself to be loved into existence by the Father and loving absolutely in return: "As the Father has loved me, so I have loved you; abide in my love. If you keep my commandments, you will abide in my love, just as I have kept my Father's commandments and abide in his love. I have said these things to you so that my joy may be in you, and that your joy may be complete" (John 15:9–11).

I've been suggesting, then, that in the Farewell Discourses we hear Jesus initiating his disciples into a sharing in trinitarian life, that is, into his relationship with the Father—joyfully fulfilled within them by the Holy Spirit. The word that Jesus asks us to keep and that only the Spirit can make resound within our common life; this word is the true depth and meaning of God's intention, God's idea, for us and for each creature. And, as we've said, this Word turns out—as we see from its Incarnation—to be nothing less than full relationship with God as God's own beloved; that is, God's "idea" of us and calling forth of us into existence: "to all who received him [the Word of God], who believed in his name, he gave power to become children of God" (John 1:13).

Given the world's form of relations, dominated by power and fear, Jesus' form of relation is rejected. But Jesus makes of the world's fear and rejection of love a way to express the fullest love possible, the creative love that is the meaning of all things: on the cross he refuses to cease loving but goes on entrusting himself to those he loved and to the Father's loving of himself and them in him. As the contemporary Anglican theologian John Milbank puts it, though Christ's offering of himself is "unto death, the death that the Logos dies is a showing, within a death-dreaming cosmos, of that utter ecstatic self-giving which is eternal life itself."[2] The ecstatic giving of eternal life, the overflowing availability of the Divine Persons one to another, becomes visible in our "death-dreaming cosmos" as the prodigal abandon of Jesus' free self-giving to others in his life and in his death. And the everlasting acceptance and delight in this eternal giving becomes visible in our world as the new life of Jesus beyond any dominion of death, and as the outpouring of the Spirit upon those who receive him.

In the Farewell Discourses we hear Jesus preparing the disciples to enter into the meaning of his passion and death. Not surprisingly, the church is especially attentive to these passages during the Easter season, when the Spirit whom Jesus breathes upon his friends inspires within the church a growing realization of our calling and true identity: for this is the Spirit of the Father's infinitely giving love, the Spirit of our adoption into Christ's filial relationship with the Father. Another way to put this is to say that, in the Incarnation and the Passion, God has assumed our death-dealing divisions into the life-bearing differences, the relational communion, of the Divine Persons. And in Easter and Pentecost, God has begun to pour out the power of this relation between Jesus and the Father into our world, converting our dividedness into communion. It is crucial here to see that Jesus does not fulfill his mission by any achievement in the world: if he had wanted a purely human gift to be given us he could have done so. But he knows himself to live from and for an infinitely giving life, a life that passes beyond the barriers of anything we can know as life and even beyond what we experience as death. And Jesus accepts to be, in his folly and weakness, a sign of this divine wisdom and strength that exceed all the limits of sinful existence. That is why he does not reconcile us by a sterling human achievement of his own, but by holding our condition, in himself, out to the hands of the Father. Only in this way could he fully assume our divisions and bitterness and bear them up into the peaceful self-giving and differentiation of the Trinity. As the Dominican theologian Herbert McCabe writes:

> Jesus knows he is not going to live to establish the Kingdom. He did not transform the world; the colonial society went on as before; the same kinds of bitterness and meanness and hatreds went on as before. In death on the cross he handed over all the meaning of his human life to the Father; this is his prayer. The Father has not accomplished his will through any success of Jesus; Jesus is left with nothing but his love and his obedience, and this is the prayer to

the Father to work through his failure. And, of course, the answer to that prayer is the resurrection, when the Father through the dead but risen Christ does accomplish his loving will for human creatures. Through the risen Christ the Spirit is poured out upon all men, or, to put it another way, the relationship between Jesus and the Father, between the Son and the Father, is extended to all men. Before his death Jesus had tried, but in the end failed, to bring the Spirit of love to a small group of disciples; now through him the Father pours the Spirit throughout the world; by this the world is to be transformed into a community of love, the Kingdom of God.[3]

Or as St. Paul says, "In Christ God was reconciling the world to himself" (2 Cor. 5:19). The church itself is meant to be the germ, the preliminary sign, of this reconciling action; for there, by grace, the divisions and enmities and sinful alienations that characterize the world are overtaken and caught up within the peaceful self-sharing of the Divine Persons which is the foundation of the church's life. As McCabe puts it just above, through the risen Christ and his Body the Church the Holy Spirit (the relation between Jesus and the Father) is extended throughout the world, and "by this the world is to be transformed into a community of love."

Perhaps, as a final note, we could consider the spiritual implications of this theology, observing the particular stance it invites us to take. First, it calls us to a passionate listening for and discernment of God's living Word as it resounds uniquely in each situation; attending in fidelity to what might be God's idea or purpose in every circumstance. This would mean a constant prayer to love Christ the more, so as to know him more deeply, and thereby to align ourselves in each moment more clearly with his mission. And second, this theology calls us to an equally passionate freedom for God to move us beyond what we have understood or accomplished. As Jesus surrendered his life work into the hands of the One he trusted, precisely so that the Father could pour out an infinitely greater gift, so are we called to pray for a continually growing availability to God's unfathomable desire. In this way the Spirit may unfold within our contexts the ever-greater meaning of the Father's love, sometimes requiring from us a costly trust and hope in God's purposes beyond our imagining. As the Anglican theologian Austin Farrer once put it:

> More than all we ask for will be granted, if two conditions are present: first, a passionate concern for what we conceive the will of God to be; and second, an entire submission to the will of God, as God actually means it to be. How hard it is, to be strongly concerned for the will of God as we think we know it; and yet so detached from our conception of it, that we rejoice to have our purpose transformed by the overruling of God's hand.[4]

Yet even in those moments of overruling we need never be fearful but may be hopeful and glad, for the one who takes us beyond where we had thought to go has called us friends.

Notes

1. Gregory of Nyssa, *Commentary on the Song of Songs,* Homily 11, trans. Casimir McCambley, ocso (Brookline, Mass.: Hellenic College Press, 1987), 201. On the significant use of this theme of divine infinity as a guide to theological method, see Lewis Ayres's illuminating discussion of it in the supporters of Nicene orthodoxy: Ayres, *Nicaea and Its Legacy: An Approach to Fourth-Century Trinitarian Theology* (Oxford: Oxford University Press, 2004), chapter 11, "On the Contours of Mystery," 273–301.

2. John Milbank, *Being Reconciled: Ontology and Pardon* (London and New York: Routledge, 2003), 100.

3. Herbert McCabe, *God Matters* (London: Geoffrey Chapman, 1987), 99–100.

4. Austin Farrer, "The Transforming Will," a sermon in *The End of Man* by the same author (London: SPCK, 1973), 106.

A Letter from a Friend

Jenny Te Paa

My dear Frank,

When I was asked to contribute to a collection of essays in your honor I was so very deeply touched. Then, I was momentarily perplexed at receiving a further message from the publishers of this precious text, for here I relearned an old literary descriptive, one I had not seen for many years—*festschrift!* I confess, I had to look in my dictionary for precise meaning and here I found: *festschrift—a volume of learned articles or essays by colleagues and admirers, serving as a tribute or memorial especially to a scholar.*

Forgive me, Frank, that this is neither a learned article nor necessarily an essay, but it is most definitely a very warm and loving tribute not simply to a scholar but to a consummate priest, bishop, and man of God. It comes from one indescribably proud to be known as colleague, admirer, and, I trust, as friend.

At times like this, as with any tribute, one is tempted to adopt a chronological approach—*you* know, the one that begins, "I have had the honor of knowing Frank for so many years . . . ," whereas it occurs to me that the length of time we have been friends and colleagues is actually irrelevant. I simply give thanks to God for introducing us to one another, and for the very special moments of conversation and of prayer that we have been able to enjoy as we have each sought in different ways to fulfill our individual commitment to always be faithfully and humbly in God's service.

As you know, I have been involved in university-level theological education for many years now, and I also know you are aware that I have developed a fairly uncompromising and unapologetically critical view of the behavior and attitudes of many of those in leadership positions in our beloved church. I don't know if I ever shared what follows with you before, Frank, but let me do so now because I think it will cause you to smile that gentle, self-effacing smile of yours!

Before November 2003, as I worked on various Anglican boards, commissions, and networks at both national and international levels, I would often find myself distractedly wondering just where certain people gained their theological credentials, let alone their ministry skills. As I sat in gatherings usually dominated by the ordained stream of church leaders and as discussions evolved around the concerns of the moment—whether to do with peace and justice, theological education, doctrine, women's rights, youth ministry, poverty, and so on—I would find myself increasingly discomfited at the ever-apparent paucity of ordained church leaders who could bring to the discussions careful, compassionate, and credible theological insight. Of course I immediately recognized the theological educational implications of all that I was witnessing, and so to comfort myself I started imagining how glorious it would be to have the privilege of theologically re-educating those "in need"! I imagined a globally representative classroom, and I started making a short-list (well, it was originally intended to be just a list but somehow it did end up a rather short one) of those I would call upon to help me teach should I ever be in charge of such a classroom. Without equivocation, Frank, you were right there on my very short list as one whose own unerring example of extraordinarily tender, grace-filled, gently good-humored, public prophetic witness was already a source of inspiration, of encouragement, and of deep reassurance to many Anglicans all over God's world. You have consistently modeled in your being as a bishop *"sensible, respectable, hospitable, what it means to be an apt teacher . . . ."* An "apt teacher" indeed, and this was before November 2003, and the consecration as Bishop of New Hampshire a man living in a committed relationship with another man.

My dear friend, it has not gone unnoticed by those of us who love and respect you that even since November 2003—a period when God alone knows how unbelievably testing life has been for you—you have continued to model not only the very best of who you have been called by God to be, but you have incontrovertibly superseded all reasonable expectations, especially given the tumultuous circumstances that have at times engulfed you so unfairly and with such unbearable intensity. That God would see fit in the near future to bless the lives of students with such exceptional "aptness" has now become my fervent prayer.

When we met in New York earlier in 2005 during the United Nations Consultation on the Status of Women, you had recently returned from the Primates' Meeting in Northern Ireland. I had heard from friends of the refusal of some of your brother primates to break bread with you. I have already spoken publicly of this because it troubles me deeply as one who so proudly belongs to a church that, in turn, prides itself on the centrality of the sacraments, especially of the Eucharist as perhaps the most tangible symbol of our oneness in Christ. I cannot begin to comprehend the theology (or lack thereof) at work in the hearts of those who would deny to anyone, even themselves, Eucharistic hospitality. What touched me so deeply when we met was that though you named the reality of what had occurred, you never once spoke of what it was like to be personally vilified so blatantly and doubtless to be deeply hurt as a result.

In my discussions with many of our friends in common, they too report that throughout the entire post–New Hampshire period you have demonstrated an unwavering attitude of deep magnanimity toward all of your episcopal peers, especially those who have so publicly insulted or rejected you. It is this powerful combination of your fearless naming of iniquitous behavior, your boundless generosity of spirit, and your insistence on unconditional forgiveness that has further endeared you to us all. As well, your example has undeniably served as the most unexpectedly effective discipleship teaching tool you could ever have imagined employing. I mean, how on earth do you expect that your friends could possibly ignore your example? Our mantra to ourselves has become: *Gee, if Frank can stay dignified and calm in the face of all he has had to endure, then what is our excuse for not acting similarly especially when, thanks be to God, we have no experience of what he must have suffered!*

I have another very poignant memory, which is of a

meeting held at Kanuga Conference Center in North Carolina in mid-2004. You were there as leader of a small group from within ECUSA who had been asked to meet with the Lambeth Commission on Communion, of which I was a member, and which produced the Windsor Report. You may recall that during our meeting I asked you what sense you had of the extent to which those outside the United States were erroneously (albeit understandably) conflating their extremely negative views of U.S. foreign policy with an ill-informed and selectively negative view of ECUSA. In other words, I was asking you if you saw an unfortunate link being made between the increasing global perception of U.S. imperialism in foreign policy as an unwelcome and uninvited and often irresistible imposition, and U.S./ECUSA "imperialism" in matters of human sexuality as an unwelcome and scripturally indefensible imposition. Your reaction to my question caused me a brief moment of anxiety. Initially I sensed that perhaps you had received it as an accusation rather than a genuine enquiry. However, your humble and measured response evoked from me, and from some of my colleagues on that day, a tremendous sense of respect for you. You explained, amongst other important things, the structural reality of ECUSA. Your explanation made very clear the limitations of your own role as Presiding Bishop and therefore your inability to act with any level of imperiousness, even had you wished to! On occasions such as this it would have been so easy for you to be justifiably impatient because at least some members of the Lambeth Commission ought to have known of the structural constraints ourselves. But no, you did not give even a hint of impatience; you took your time, and with grace and care you simply explained all you could to help us understand.

My friend, in spite of efforts to derail, or at least to seriously subvert, your episcopal leadership in recent times, it has been inspirational to witness your ongoing involvement in such a tremendous range of inter-faith, ecumenical, and inter-provincial work. It has been wonderful to see you actively maintaining the broad spread of interest you have always had in God's people all over the world. In particular, it has been a source of incalculable reassurance to see you continuing to work with tenacity and unerring pastoral devotion for projects and for people whose ministry, like your own, is to support the healing and flourishing of those least advantaged in the global village. It is as though you have found the miraculous means of grace by which to transcend obstacles placed in the way of the work of mission and ministry to which God has so irrefutably called you.

Well Frank, there it is—just a few reflective thoughts by way of a loving tribute from me, your South Pacific sister, at this time of your preparing to journey on beyond the years of your call to the Office of Presiding Bishop. As with any major transition there will doubtless be moments of grieving, of relief, of uncertainty at what the future may hold, of frustration at work incomplete, of exhilaration at new-found freedom from responsibility, and of quiet joy at considering new possibilities for yourself and for Phoebe and your family. Please know as you move inexorably through the inevitable processes of change, that you are being constantly upheld in the prayers of so many all over God's infinitely glorious world who love and care very deeply for you and for those dearest to you.

*Loving God, we give thanks for the ministry of
Frank Griswold, for his gracious and dignified
leadership, for his clear and compassionate modeling
of Jesus' call to discipleship. We ask at this time that
you would bless Frank and Phoebe and their family with an abundance of your spirit of peace and of
your gentle healing mercy. Reassure the Griswold
family of their very special place in the hearts of so
many throughout the worldwide Anglican Communion and beyond in ecumenical and inter-faith
constituencies. Embrace your servant leader Frank,
with wisdom to know, instinct to act, and with un-
equivocal love to share with all who are so utterly
privileged to be blessed, indeed, to be touched by his
extraordinary ministry. Amen.*

With love and affection to you and to Phoebe—ma
te Atua korua e manaaki, e tiaki i nga wa katoa.

Arohanui,

Jenny

A Challenge for Seminaries: Preparing Leaders for a Ministry of Reconciliation

Martha Horne

T HE COMMENT CAME at the end of a heated discussion about clergy and congregations seeking episcopal oversight from diocesan bishops in other parts of the Anglican Communion. What began as a question of canon law and Anglican polity quickly jumped like summer brush fires from one "hot button" issue to another. Tempers flared, accusations were made, and battle lines were drawn. In a community often noted for its hospitality, an air of unmistakable hostility hung over the group. Wading into the fray, a visitor asked innocently, "What would it take to reconcile the differences among you?" It was then that an angry student replied scornfully, "Reconciliation is not the issue here. The issue is faithfulness to God's word. When it comes to obeying God's will, there can be no room for compromise. I'm not interested in reconciliation with someone who refuses to obey God's word."

It was a sobering moment. Somehow, I remember thinking, we have failed this student. Why does he believe that a call for reconciliation is a call for compromise, or an attempt to sidestep the word of God? How could he be in seminary and not know that reconciliation is God's own work; work that God has initiated, accomplished, and called us to share? It became clear to me then that those who are preparing for leadership in our church must be deeply grounded in biblical and theological understandings of the doctrine of reconciliation if they are to be faithful and effective leaders. That is particularly true in times of conflict.

The invitation to participate in this festschrift in honor of our Presiding Bishop has caused me to think again about that heated exchange that took place in the seminary where I serve as Dean and President. It was one of those "teachable moments" when students are challenged to examine their assumptions and behavior in light of Christian teaching and practice. In this instance, a volatile and potentially divisive discussion provided an opportunity for theological reflection on reconciliation. That reflection, in turn, led to a renewed commitment to the common life of the seminary.

Reconciliation has been a central theme in Frank Griswold's preaching and teaching as Presiding Bishop. Again and again, through one difficult time after another, he has repeatedly called us to remember that God has already done the costly work of reconciliation. Like the apostle Paul (no stranger to conflict himself), Bishop Griswold has called the church to participate in Christ's ministry of reconciliation.

The seminaries of our church are a unique resource for equipping leaders for the ministry of reconciliation. Seminaries face many challenges in preparing men and women for positions of leadership in our church.

Some people seem to think that theological education is a luxury the church can no longer afford; others believe that seminaries are out of touch with the realities and challenges facing congregations today. Diocesan Conventions and General Convention routinely receive and often adopt resolutions about what seminaries should be doing: training in ecumenical relations and evangelism, workshops on sexual misconduct, anti-racism training, treatment of substance abuse, and Spanish-language training are but a few. Conflict resolution is among the specific skills frequently identified as important by bishops and congregational leaders. Yet despite the current climate of conflict and division within our church, there has been little call for deep, theologically informed reflection on God's reconciling work in the world, as revealed in the pages of Scripture and in the lives of faithful individuals and communities throughout the centuries.

A well-rounded, biblically grounded seminary curriculum provides unique resources for those called to a ministry of reconciliation. Preparation for that ministry takes place in the seminary's formal, or "explicit," curriculum, through courses in Scripture, church history, theology, ethics and moral theology, liturgics, homiletics, pastoral care, and the practice of ministry. It also takes place in the more informal, "implicit" curriculum of community life, where students and faculty of diverse views work together in an environment of prayer, study, and fellowship characterized by respectful discourse, charity, and civility. It is not possible, in these few pages, to illustrate all the ways in which a seminary curriculum prepares leaders for a ministry of reconciliation. What follows are a series of snapshots of various points in a seminary curriculum where the study of different theological disciplines can provide important knowledge and skills for a ministry of reconciliation.

For all Christians, a serious study of reconciliation begins within the pages of Scripture. Study begins with an examination of the word itself, and a review of its use in Hebrew and Christian Scriptures. A survey of pertinent texts in Hebrew Scriptures yields a smattering of different Hebrew words, all of which have something to do with the act of atonement. A similar study of New Testament passages examines pertinent texts in Matthew and other gospels. It is in the writings of the apostle Paul, however, that an explicit theological doctrine of reconciliation begins to appear. Space does not permit here a thorough examination of Pauline, much less biblical, understandings of reconciliation. Yet much can be learned from even a quick look at what many believe to be one of the most illustrative biblical texts, found in Paul's second letter to the church at Corinth: "Therefore, if anyone is in Christ, he is a new creation; the old has passed away. All this is from God, who through Christ reconciled us to himself and gave us the ministry of reconciliation; that is, Christ was reconciling the world to himself, not counting their trespasses against them, and entrusting to us the ministry of reconciliation. So we are ambassadors for Christ, God making his appeal through us. We beseech you on behalf of Christ, be reconciled to God" (2 Cor. 5:17–20).

With a remarkable economy of words, Paul presents two central themes in his teaching on reconciliation: 1) reconciliation is an act of God, brought about by God's initiative ("all this is from God"), and not by human actions; and 2) we have been entrusted with the ministry of reconciliation, so that God's reconciling work, accomplished in Christ, has ongoing witness in the life of the church. The verb Paul uses to speak of reconciliation is *katalasso*. It appears six times in his writings: in five instances the term refers clearly to the relationship between God and humans; only once is it used to speak of relationships between human beings (1 Cor. 7:11). As Christoph Schwobel has noted, "The characteristic feature of the use of the word in Paul and the Pauline school is its predominantly theological character; reconciliation is defined in a theological context and not developed analogically from interpersonal human relationships."[1] Students learn, therefore, that a biblical understanding of reconciliation begins with an understanding of God as author and agent, thereby dismissing any notion of reconciliation as merely a human activity or strategy.

Using the tools and methodologies for critical word study and exegesis, the student then delves deeper into the passage, examining key phrases: "a new creation," for example. What did this mean for Paul and the church at Corinth? "All this is from God," Paul writes; what is the "all this"? By a careful, word-by-word, phrase-by-phrase study of the passage, a doctrine of reconciliation emerges from the text, one that connects the work of reconciliation with the great biblical themes of creation, atonement, redemption, salvation, grace, and finally, with a ministry that has been entrusted to us.

Paul then turns his attention to the church's responsibility to proclaim and practice reconciliation. The church is the community of women and men who are entrusted with that ministry, who are "ambassadors," or agents of God's reconciling work. As God has chosen not to count our transgressions against us, but has, instead, restored us to communion with God, so we should deal with our fellow human beings. Paul's teaching here is both theological and ethical, addressed to the fractious Christian community in Corinth. His ethical teaching flows from his theological conviction; because God has chosen to reconcile us and to restore our broken relationship with God, we have a responsibility to *act* as people who have received this great gift of forgiveness. Reconciliation, as understood in Paul's theology, always has implications for how one lives a Christian life. A comprehensive seminary curriculum integrates an understanding of the biblical foundations of reconciliation with ethical reflection and with development of skills for preaching and pastoral care.

Having provided the tools for a careful mining of biblical texts that speak of reconciliation, the seminary curriculum invites students into a conversation with those in other generations who have pondered the meaning of reconciliation. How have some of our church's great thinkers and leaders understood reconciliation? What circumstances in the life of the church have provided occasions for further development of the church's ministry of reconciliation?

The history of the church is full of such occasions, as even a cursory study quickly demonstrates. Robert L. Browning and Roy A. Reed draw attention to several such instances in their book *Forgiveness, Reconciliation, and Moral Courage*: How, for example, would bishops of the third century respond to those who had fallen away from the church during the persecutions of Christians by Roman authorities, then later sought readmission to the church? That situation led Cyprian, bishop of

Carthage, to develop a process of penance, confession, and forgiveness, leading to a liturgy of reconciliation and restoration of communion for those who earlier turned away. Future generations would continue to develop and refine rituals as sacramental expressions of God's reconciling love, reminding us of the powerful ways in which our liturgies convey God's grace. Martin Luther's life-changing encounter with Paul's teaching that we, as sinners, are justified by God's grace (Rom. 3:23–24) profoundly shaped his own understanding of the doctrine of reconciliation and his contempt for the ways in which the church's practices regarding the sale of indulgences had distorted biblical teachings.[2] Study of our church's history reminds us that we are not the first to struggle with the difficult work of reconciliation. Insights from our past shed light on our present and offer hope for finding a way forward. Ancient liturgies, appropriated and sometimes adapted for current circumstances, help to convey words of confession and forgiveness, both necessary for reconciliation.

In recent years the work of the Truth and Reconciliation Commission (TRC) of the government of South Africa has made great contributions to our understanding of reconciliation. Established in 1995 in an attempt to foster peaceful coexistence among the people of South Africa, following years of racial apartheid and injustice, the TRC acknowledged the need for people to be able to tell their stories before healing and reconciliation could occur. As the people of South Africa sought ways to make their way forward, the desire for revenge that many victims felt was set aside in favor of trying to understand what happened in the past, in order to create a better and more peaceful society for the future. Victims were given the chance to tell their stories in public hearings, enabling them to give voice to the atrocities committed against them and their families, while also allowing listeners to grasp the extent of suffering that apartheid had imposed on fellow human beings. Reconciliation was possible only after people had spoken and heard the truth of what had actually happened. The implications for pastoral care as well as justice are enormous, as we seek reconciliation among those who have been the victims of abuse and oppression.

Many valuable lessons have emerged through South Africa's reflections on the work of the TRC:[3]

- Reconciliation involves the healing of old wounds, and that healing takes time. The wounds need to be re-opened in order to drain and heal.
- Reconciliation needs to occur not only between individuals, but within and among communities.
- Reconciliation needs to begin on a local level, as many in South Africa observed, where people know each other.[4]
- Reconciliation requires us to speak and to hear the truth.
- Reconciliation is hard work.
- Reconciliation requires us to set aside our preconceived notions of justice.

As Charles Villa-Vicencio, former Director of the research department of the TRC, writes of its work: "Reconciliation involves a different kind of justice that does not seek revenge, but that also does not countenance impunity. This kind of justice allows both for the capacity for evil and the capacity for good that resides within humanity. It accepts moral and political responsibility for redressing the needs of victims, as well as the need to ensure that perpetrators become responsible members of society."[5] Insights gained from the experience of the TRC remind us of the complexities and ambiguities of the human condition.

Reconciliation is a complex process that resists simplistic definitions. But as so often happens with complex concepts, there is a popular tendency to reduce them to simplistic, often trivialized remnants. Dietrich Bonhoeffer warned us against the desire for "cheap grace," citing the costly nature of God's grace, so freely bestowed upon us.[6]

In a similar way, theologian Jean Bethke Elshtain warns us against the dangers of trivializing the hard work of forgiveness needed for reconciliation to occur: "We are awash in confession these days. There is the low form of daytime television talk shows and the slightly higher form in bookstores. Rectitude has given way to 'contrition chic,' as one wag called it, meaning a bargain-basement way to gain publicity, sympathy, and even absolution by trafficking in one's status as a victim or victimizer."[7] She laments the ways in which our culture "traffics in and cheapens notions of forgiveness ('let's put this behind us' or 'let's achieve closure')."[8] Yet forgiveness, she maintains, is an essential ingredient in the reconciliation of political conflicts. Drawing on the experience of Catholics in Northern Ireland, she cites the example of Cardinal Cahal Daly, who in a sermon preached at Canterbury Cathedral asked for forgiveness for the "wrongs and hurts inflicted by Irish people upon the people of this country on many occasions ... I believe that this reciprocal recognition of the need to forgive and to be forgiven is a necessary condition for proper Christian, and human, and indeed, political relationships between our two islands in the future."[9] Reconciliation, we learn, is not just about one's relationship with God, or with another individual; it has social and political implications, as well.

With their insistence that forgiveness is central to reconciliation, Elshtain and Cardinal Daly bring us back to where we began—back to the apostle Paul and his recognition of God's forgiveness as the first step in the divine act of reconciliation. It is the place where our church needs to return, again and again, in our life together. Christian life calls us continually to recognize the injuries we inflict on others, to respond in genuine contrition, and to ask forgiveness for our sins of commission and omission. These disciplines of faith are learned in congregations, but practiced with greater regularity in the context of a seminary where students, faculty, and staff share a common life of worship, study, and fellowship. Far from being the ivory towers, distanced from the occupations and cares of the world, as many seem to think, seminaries are laboratories where its residents struggle daily with what it means to live in love and charity with our neighbors. Self-examination, confession, and forgiveness are practiced not only in our liturgies, but also in our common life.

Now, more than ever, our church needs leaders who are deeply grounded in biblical, historical, and theological understandings of reconciliation, and who understand their implications for ethics, proclamation, and pastoral care. Frank Griswold's ministry has borne witness to his own understanding of the depth and richness of Christian teaching about reconciliation as an act of God, on our behalf, and a ministry to which God has called us. He has been a strong supporter of our seminaries and an articulate voice for the importance of theological education in the life of our church. In these days perhaps we might dedicate ourselves, both individually and collectively, to a renewed commitment to the ministry of reconciliation. In that way we would honor not only Frank Griswold's ministry among us, but also the God who entrusted that ministry to us.

Notes

1. Christoph Schwobel, "Reconciliation: From Biblical Observations to Dogmatic Reconstruction," in Colin E. Gunton, ed., *The Theology of Reconciliation* (London: T. & T. Clark, Ltd., 2003), 16.

2. Robert L. Browning and Roy A. Reed, *Forgiveness, Reconciliation, and Moral Courage* (Grand Rapids: Eerdmans, 2004), 102–115.

3. For a full discussion of these lessons, see Hugo van der Merwe, "National and Community Reconciliation: Competing Agendas in the South African Truth and Reconciliation Commission" and Charles Villa-Vicencio, "Restorative Justice in Social Context: The South African Truth and Reconciliation Commission," in Nigel Biggar, ed., *Burying the Past: Making Peace and Doing Justice after Civil Conflict* (Washington, D.C.: Georgetown University Press, 2003).

4. Hugo Van der Merwe, in Biggar, op. cit., 114.

5. Charles Villa-Vicencio, in Biggar, op. cit., 249.

6. Dietrich Bonhoeffer, *The Cost of Discipleship*.

7. Jean Bethke Elshtain, "Politics and Forgiveness," in Biggar, op. cit., 45.

8. Ibid., 45.

9. Ibid., 52.

The Church as an Agent of Reconciliation: A Practical View

Brian J. Grieves

What in me—in the church—needs to be repaired and transformed in order for me—for us—to enter wholeheartedly into God's work of repairing the world?

FRANK T. GRISWOLD

The Locus of Mission

A young priest once was asked how he defined the mission of the church. In response he quoted a seminary professor's remark to a group of clergy: "Jesus didn't come to start a church. He came to usher in the Reign of God." The professor was the Rev. Dr. Massey H. Shepherd, legendary teacher of liturgics and often noted as an architect of the 1979 Book of Common Prayer. The quotation doesn't quite define mission; it does point to where mission is to be carried out, and it is not in the church.

Archbishop Njongonkulu Ndungane, primate of the Province of Southern Africa, has often said that "Jesus didn't come to save the church. He came to save the world." Taking the two quotations together, we clearly see that mission is carried out in the world where we are to establish God's reign. That is, the church is an agent for mission, not the focus.

Thus, salvation of the world is the focus of mission and surely salvation of the world is desperately needed. This has always been true, of course. In every age we have seen war and conflict, poverty and injustice, oppression and discrimination, hunger and suffering, abuse of power and threats to the environment and all God has created. There have been challenges for every generation, including our own, and responding in accordance with the values of the gospel is our mission.

Divergent Views of the Church

In every age the faithful have different views of how their faith might best be expressed in the world. These varying ecclesiologies were certainly apparent in the late 1960s, when attending seminary provided particular challenges, certainly at the Church Divinity School of the Pacific where I was a student. CDSP is located just one block from the University of California campus where then-Governor Ronald Reagan sent in the National Guard to quell anti-Vietnam war protests. The Dean ventured onto the sidewalk to ask the troops please to stay off the seminary grass. The troops stayed off the grass, but the clash over the Vietnam War spilled onto the seminary campus and affected community life. Some were ardent opponents of the war, while others thought politics and church don't mix. The students were described as those who marched and those who prayed. Such a division, then and now, hampers the church's mission. These events provide a clear example of a dynamic that is part of our church's life and is expressed in the circumstances of each period.

In these current days the Episcopal Church has made a formal commitment through the General Convention to work toward growing the church and increasing membership. Even so, there are those who believe that the emphasis on growth diminishes the focus on the church's mission. This reveals an unhelpful division of church members into those who emphasize mission and those who emphasize evangelism. Differently stated, some focus on Jesus' love for us as a personal savior while others put a priority on living out the imperatives he gave us. The two belong together. It is not either/or, but both/and. Evangelism and mission are two sides of the same coin.

For obvious reasons, mission is served by increasing membership. More hands and feet (and indeed financial resources) strengthen the mission. When we fail to work for growth, or ignore decline, we do so at the peril of mission. However, the effort to increase numbers by itself is insufficient. We must ask: why do we want to grow the church? There might be many legitimate answers, but none trumps this one: we want to spread the saving message of the gospel and thus draw others into participating in God's mission.

Though embarrassingly fallible, made up as it is of fallible human beings, the church is a great and sacred mystery. It is the life of the gathered community, through prayer and liturgy and our growing up together into Christ, that nurtures and prepares us for the work of mission. Nevertheless, we must be cautious in making the church the object of our worship, or in seeking it only as a refuge, lest we forget it is the *world* that Jesus loved and came to save and heal.

What, Then, is the Mission?

Americans live in a post 9/11 world, but the problems of violence, poverty, and injustice didn't begin September 11, 2001. Though the context may have been altered and the American psyche damaged, the problems were always there. Even so, the destruction of the Twin Towers was a wrenching, almost surreal, sight on that clear and sunny Tuesday morning in New York City. The chapel at the Episcopal Church Center was crowded that day, not only with staff, but with visitors who poured in off the streets. The Presiding Bishop was celebrant and preacher. In a rare moment of public emotion, Bishop Griswold banged the pulpit and demanded, "How many more innocent people will lose their lives as a consequence of these actions today!?"[1] He invited us to participate with all our hearts and minds and strength in God's project of reconciliation, and warned against a national strategy of retaliation. As we now know, retaliation was to be the course. And, the answer to his prophetic question has been arriving in the statistics of news reports almost every day since.

In the first days after that disaster, Griswold launched a call for reconciliation. Quoting from the catechism in the Book of Common Prayer, he reminded the church that "the mission of the church is to restore all people to unity with God and each other in Christ.... The Church pursues its mission as it prays and worships, proclaims the Gospel, and promotes justice, peace and love." Over the time of his primacy he has repeatedly challenged the Episcopal Church to be about this task.

The catechism reminds us that mission is carried out "through the ministry of all its members," and that reconciliation—that is, "to restore all people to unity"—lies at the heart of mission. The work of reconciliation is to heal divisions among people, bind the wounds within the created order, build understanding among different cultures, religions, and peoples, and promote justice and peace.

Said another way, reconciliation is found in our charge to be stewards. At its heart, stewardship is about how we reconcile the brokenness of creation. Stewardship of financial resources and the raising of funds are means to that end. However, the human community is called to be the steward not simply of the church, but of the earth.

Justice is a prerequisite for reconciliation, and God's justice is not necessarily what we might imagine it to be. Bishop Griswold, in his series of homilies in *Going Home,* says "God's justice and righteousness consist of the ordering of all things according to God's own imagination and desire."[2] Discerning God's imagination is a challenging task, taking us out of ourselves and putting us into the mind of God.

The Reign of God will be achieved when there is reconciliation among all peoples and the Creator, when relationships are restored at last and the earth is at peace.

Some years ago, following the Rwandan genocide, Bishop James Ottley, then the Anglican Observer at the United Nations, went to Rwanda to see how the work of reconciliation was present in that traumatized land. The strongest word he heard was that before there could be reconciliation, there must be justice. It was inconceivable to the survivors of the genocide that there could be any reconciliation with those who committed the atrocities until there was justice.

As the Church seeks to discern what God's justice requires in our global community, we know that justice is the pre-condition that must be in place before we, the global community, can turn to one another with an embrace that will, at last, hail the establishment of the Reign of God.

Reconciliation, Christian Divisions, and Partisan Politics

There are faithful Episcopalians who have been inadequately exposed to the rationale for a Christian voice at the table where public policies are forged. This lack of imformation might lead them to criticize the church for involvement in the political arena and to wonder at the reason for the presence of the Episcopal Church's Office of Government Relations in Washington, D.C.

There are others who well understand the role of the church in matters of social policy. For them, the task is to remain grounded in the theology of mission that drives their efforts so as not to drift into simply espousing a political agenda.

It is fortunate that in the United States context there is often a common view among the mainline denominations on matters of social policy. Mainline denominations pursue a non-partisan agenda, promoting reconciliation by working toward social policies that champion civil rights for all people, equality for women, the end of poverty, environmental stewardship, and development abroad. And the list goes on.

The Episcopal Church is that strange animal that has been called the Republican Party at prayer and at the same time accused of advocating social policies that look like the platform of the Democratic Party. Neither is true, though one might assume that most Republicans and all Episcopalians do pray. And, positions advocated by the Episcopal Church through the General Convention and Executive Council arise from an adherence to gospel values, not political platforms.

Reconciliation, the Middle East, and the Role of Religions

Mission is not only impeded by divisions within the Christian community, but the world of religion itself is often marred by actions that are the antithesis of reconciliation. Among Christians, Jews, and Muslims, the children of Abraham, the failure to promote peace and justice is starkly evident. The war in Iraq is but one example of actions contrary to the views of many Christians. And sadly, as the vocabulary of faith is usurped in support of violent behavior, President Bush and Senator John McCain appeared together to defend the Iraq war as a conflict between good and evil. Senator McCain said the war is a fight "between a just regard for human dignity and a malevolent force that defiles an honorable religion by disputing God's love for each soul on Earth. It's a fight between right and wrong, good and evil. It's no more ambiguous than that."

While Senator McCain is right that Islam—the religion to which he presumably refers—is being misused, he fails to consider that perhaps Christianity is also being defiled and faith language being used to condone violence. God's name is being invoked by some Muslims to justify a "holy war" (surely one of the great oxymorons of all time), by some Jews to condone a brutal occupation in pursuit of yet more land from the Palestinian people, and by some Christians to condone a military adventure in Iraq. Bishop Griswold, in warning against an invasion of Iraq, called upon the United States, as the superpower, to act instead as super servant.

Certainly not all who believe in the Iraq war are extremists; however, in each of the three Abrahamic faiths there are extremists who justify violence in the name of their particular religion. Surely this sets up a strange contradiction. For Christians, we know that Jesus rejected violence when he submitted himself to the Roman guards in Gethsemane, rebuking Peter for wielding his sword. The Episcopal Church has long been on record as saying, in the words of the Lambeth Conference and adopted by General Convention, that "war, as a means of settling international disputes, is incompatible with the Gospel of Jesus Christ." War, from the perspective of any of the three Abrahamic faith groups, represents a failure of the human spirit.

It would appear that the whole human family has turned in on itself in a reckless age of violence, hatred, rage, arrogance, and self-righteousness, and that the three Abrahamic faiths, rather than being a solution, are part of the fabric of the problems we face as a global community. No one is blameless. The war in Iraq and the Israeli/Palestinian conflict are as much a failure of the faith community as of political leaders. If we are to be about the work of reconciliation, Jews, Christians, and Muslims must find a common voice to say no to violence and fanaticism perpetuated in the name of God.

One More Word

The Griswold years have been marked by a challenge to the church that emerged after the tragedy of 9/11 to engage in the work of mission, that is, God's project of reconciliation. This is the task for every generation. It is not meant to be done only by a local church committee or a diocesan task force or through a church office. This is the vocation to which all the baptized are called.

As noted earlier, every congregation from time to time might do well to review the question: What is our mission? In so doing, we discover not only what we are to do, but who we are. As Bishop Griswold has said, "The very terms of our mission, our particular function within the context of God's ongoing work of reconciliation—as limbs and members of Christ's body—draw us ever more deeply into the mystery of Christ, which is to discover in grace and truth who we are and who we are called to be."[3]

> Christ . . . gives us gifts as manifestations of Christ's desire that we join him in the ongoing task of binding up, setting free, and making all things new.[4]

Notes

Epigram: Frank T. Griswold, *Going Home: An Invitation to Jubilee* (Cambridge, MA: Cowley Publications, 2000), 9.

1. A man of disciplined prayer, rooted in the spirituality of the desert tradition of the fourth century, Bishop Griswold has

a passion for the mission of the church. Prayer is his grounding for that mission. He bridges the divide between those who march and those who pray. Shortly after arriving in New York, he summoned me to say that he wanted to do his part to support the many social policies of the church. He has made regular forays to Washington to visit political leaders and has never in my memory refused to stand behind a social policy of General Convention or Executive Council.

2. *Going Home*, 4.
3. Ibid., 78.
4. Ibid., 79–80.

A Small, Good Thing

Peter S. Hawkins

The Psalmist tells us, "How good and pleasant it is when kindred live together in unity!" (Ps. 133:1). What he neglects to say is how seldom this good and pleasant thing happens. The stories Scripture tells are not about coming together but rather about rupture and discord. Brothers are at lethal odds with one another, children turn against their parents, disciples fail or outright betray their master, and the "saints" at this or that Pauline church seem to have been perpetually at one another's throats. From Cain and Abel onwards, kindred behave like sworn enemies.

But then there come those rare moments of reconciliation, all the more breathtaking for being so few and far between. Think of Jacob's flight from Canaan after bamboozling his brother Esau first out of his birthright and then his blessing. After twenty years on the run, it is time to come home; but what can he possibly expect from the brother he has so terribly wronged—a brother who greets him with a massed army of four hundred men! Anticipating the worst, he puts his household of wives and children behind him, ready to face Esau on his own. In his brother's presence he bows low to the ground seven times, as do his wives and children. It is clear that someone must die, but not the little ones, perhaps only Jacob. Esau, however, is not the man he might have been. Instead of delivering a lethal blow, he runs toward Jacob and embraces him, throws his arms around his estranged brother and kisses him until they both dissolve into tears over the sheer miracle of their reunion. Jacob cannot believe his eyes, or keep from giving gifts to the one he essentially fleeced out of birthright and blessing. "For truly to see your face is like seeing the face of God," he tells his brother, "since you have received me with such favor" (Gen. 33:10 NRSV).

Jesus must have had this scene in mind when he told the parable of the Prodigal. A certain man had two sons and the younger of the two, as in the Genesis story, is the focus of attention. He wants to receive his inheritance before his father's death; he wants what he wants *now*. When he gets it, he takes the money and runs to a "far country" where everything is squandered and lost. Reduced to the status of the swine he keeps, he recalls his father's house and knows that even the slaves there have more than he. And so he returns home with a pretty speech of repentance and, perhaps, some genuine remorse. There is no time, however, for him to deliver his rehearsed words. Once his father sees him, the old man breaks decorum and runs toward the son who wandered away; his heart, we're told, is filled with compassion (Luke 15:20). Like Esau rushing toward Jacob, the father flings his arms around the wastrel, kisses him, and calls for the bestowal of gifts and a feast to celebrate the occasion. There need be no settling of accounts or scores. The simple fact of the young man's return is enough, "For this son of mine was dead and is alive again; he was lost and is found!" (v. 24).

What remains to be seen, however, is whether the Prodigal's elder brother, who enters the narrative at its midpoint, can overcome his estrangement and join the party. His resentment is understandable; it is also monumental, not only against the brother who comes home in shambles but also against the father who treats him like a king. The parable ends with questions that remain unanswered, leaving the listener or reader to provide whatever resolution there is to be. Does life trump being right or even righteousness itself? What price is worth paying so that kindred can dwell together in unity?

These stories from Genesis and Luke are deeply moving in part because they are so rare in Scripture. They touch upon wounds within the blood family, where many people experience not only the depth of human connection but also its most painful failure and loss. Is there anything more poignant, for instance, than an aged King David mourning the death of a son who had seized his kingdom and his wives? "O, my son! Absalom, my son, my son Absalom! If only I had died instead of you! O Absalom, my son, my son!" (2 Sam. 18: 33). David repeats "Absalom" and "son" again and again, as if to secure a reconciliation now made impossible by death.

It is not only the breakdown and restoration of blood relationships that tug at the heart, however. There are also those that take place between strangers, as can be seen in two related stories by Raymond Carver—"The Bath," written in the late 1970s, and its rewrite a few years later, "A Small, Good Thing."

"The Bath" is a text so radically stripped down to essentials that it stands out even in the company of Carver's other "minimalist" fictions. The story begins on a Saturday morning as a mother, Ann, goes to the bakery to order a cake for her son Scotty's birthday on the following Monday. From a loose-leaf binder of possible designs, she makes her choice—"spaceship cake"—and then leaves the baker her name and telephone number. The cake will be ready Monday morning, in plenty of time for the party that afternoon: "This was all the baker was willing to say. No pleasantries, just this small exchange, the barest information, nothing that was not necessary."[1]

This description of the baker's reticence, "nothing that was not necessary," describes the taciturn style that makes "The Bath" the eerily powerful "small exchange" that it is. Its bare plot unfolds without elaboration, as Monday morning comes and the birthday boy is hit by a car on the way to school. Scotty is taken in a coma to the hospital, where his parents keep vigil. When the father returns home for a brief rest—"fear made him want to take a bath"—he finds the telephone ringing.

> He picked up the receiver. He said, "I just got in the door!"
> "There's a cake waiting to be picked up."
> This is what the voice on the other end said.
> "What are you saying?" the father said.
> "The cake," the voice said. "Sixteen dollars."
> The husband held the receiver against his ear, trying to understand. He said, "I don't know anything about it."
> "Don't give me that," the voice said.
> The husband hung up the telephone.[2]

This non-conversation takes place between two people who do not know or care about each other. Rather, they are imprisoned in their private preoccupations, able in their mutual blindness only to hurl accusations at each other—or hang up. Similarly, the boy's parents grope for words they cannot find; the hospital staff keeps itself immune from the suffering of the couple; and Ann's one attempt to share her tragedy with other distressed parents proves to be nothing more than a matching of separate pain, as each clings to a private grief that cannot transcend personal boundaries.

At the end of the story, the mother returns home for her own attempt at respite. Once again, the telephone rings:

> "Yes!" she said. "Hello!" she said.
>
> "Mrs. Weiss," a man's voice said.
>
> "Yes," she said. "This is Mrs. Weiss. Is it about Scotty?" she said.
>
> "Scotty," the voice said. "It is about Scotty," the voice said. "It has to do with Scotty, yes."[3]

This is the way "The Bath" concludes. It is a miniature narrative that manages, despite its spare proportions, to suggest a major nightmare. Carver gives us a rapid crossfire of "she said" and "he said" with the implication of a dialogue transpiring between speakers. But there is none. Each person is hopelessly locked within a private preoccupation of his or her own: one with a dying child, the other with a birthday cake that has not been paid for or claimed. For both sides of this disembodied exchange, "It has to do with Scotty, yes." Yet this possible (but failed) bond reveals just how far each is from the other, how even the most rudimentary contact over the telephone turns into a torment. "The Bath" seems to reprise Jean-Paul Sartre's line "Hell is other people." There is no exit.

When Carver later reworked the story as "A Small, Good Thing," however, he offered his readers a way out of the impasse. At first, the difference between the two seems largely a matter of expansion. The opening interaction between mother and baker, for instance, is fleshed out to include Ann's observation that the baker is "a man old enough to be her father," that such a person "must have children who'd gone through this special time of cakes and birthday parties."[4] Likewise, the failed encounter with the other anxious folks in the hospital waiting room now becomes the occasion for a perceived connection. Ann identifies herself to the nurse as a "friend of the family," and in the midst of her own grief the reality of the other mother's sorrow becomes, at least for an instant, almost as real as her own.

Yet for all these touches of warmth, "A Small, Good Thing" also increases the horror of "The Bath," not only by multiplying the number of the baker's telephone calls but by having the last of them occur just after the couple has returned home together from the deathbed of their son. Whereas "The Bath" left us with the possibility of the boy's recovery, Carver's reworking takes that hope away. The baker's obtuseness, therefore, comes to seem almost demonic.

> "Hello," she said, and she heard something in
> the background, a humming noise. "Hello!" she
> said. "For God's sake," she said, "Who is this?
> What do you want?"
>   "Your Scotty, I got him ready for you," the
> man's voice said. "Did you forget him?"

"You evil bastard!" she shouted into the receiver. "How can you do this, you evil son of a bitch?"

"Scotty," the man said. "Have you forgotten about Scotty?" Then the man hung up on her.[5]

This final call turns the mother homicidal: "That bastard. I'd like to kill him . . . I'd like to shoot him and watch him kick."[6] In the midst of her rage, moreover, she realizes who the caller is: "That's who has the number and keeps calling us." This recognition quickly leads to a face-to-face encounter with the caller that "The Bath" never allowed—an encounter in the middle of the night when the distraught couple, dazed by a loss they cannot yet begin to absorb, rush to the bakery with a thirst for revenge. Once in the baker's presence, however, something happens to Ann:

> Just as suddenly as it had welled in her, the anger dwindled, gave way to something else, a dizzy feeling of nausea. She leaned against the wooden table that was sprinkled with flour, put her hands over her face, and began to cry, her shoulders rocking back and forth. "It isn't fair," she said. "It isn't fair."[7]

The news of the child's death, the passion of the mother, the fury that turns swiftly into vulnerability, and the sheer truth of the matter ("It isn't fair . . . It isn't fair"): all of these factors work on the baker. For the first time in the narrative, he seems to come alive. Exiting from the prison of himself, he asks the couple please to sit down. He explains himself, and as he does he takes care of them:

He spread his hands out on the table and turned them over to reveal his palms. "I don't have children myself, so I can only imagine what you must be feeling. All I can say to you now is that I'm sorry. Forgive me if you can," the baker said. "I'm not an evil man, I don't think. Not evil, like you said on the phone. You got to understand what it comes down to is I don't know how to act anymore, it would seem. Please," the man said, "let me ask you if you can find it in your hearts to forgive me?"[8]

Neither Ann nor her husband says a word at first. Instead, they allow the baker simply to feed them. "Eating is a small, good thing at a time like this," he says. And as the three of them drink his coffee and eat cinnamon rolls still hot from the oven, they give him the opportunity not only to nurture them but to speak. Whereas the story opened with the baker's refusal to talk ("just the minimum exchange of words, the necessary information"[9]), it concludes with his torrent of self-revelation. It is his isolation and loneliness that pour out—the bitter irony of constantly making "party food" but never knowing a moment's joy himself. The couple is mesmerized. Despite their exhaustion, they sit at the baker's wooden table transfixed and "careful":

> They listened to him. They ate what they could. They swallowed the dark bread. It was like daylight under the fluorescent rays of light. They talked into the early morning, the high, pale cast of light in the windows, and they did not think of leaving.[10]

With these words, "A Small, Good Thing" comes to its end, in a profound moment of communication and communion. It is as if, having shown the dividing wall of hostility between people in "The Bath," Carver then decided to dramatize (though not explain) its breaking down. The mother's desire for retribution leads to the discovery of a common broken humanity, a joining together of people formerly at odds and constantly talking past one another. Beginning with a realization of their common plight—"It isn't fair. It isn't fair"—they find a comfort in merely being together. The pain of the grieving couple opens the baker to his own torment, just as repeated request for pardon (in contrast to his succession of telephone calls) turns their accusations against him into compassion. Carver's characters begin by knowing only their separate misery. But in the end, empowered by the painful discovery of one another's lives, we see how for parents and baker alike, forgiveness can open up closed doors, can imply a future.

It may be that "A Small, Good Thing" presents its redemptive moment entirely within the realm of ordinary human knowing and becoming. No angels grace the scene, and the illumination comes from fluorescent lighting overhead. We watch as a woman's suffering releases an embittered man from his own sorrow, even as the discovery of their common plight makes possible a genuine a conversation between them. And yet, there is a curious way in which the secular graciousness of Carver's story, at least for those with eyes that see, suggests that it is underwritten by a sacred narrative, a trace of which just surfaces here. For what do we have in this meal of coffee and hot cinnamon rolls, this wooden table sprinkled with flour, this insistence of the baker that the couple take and eat—"You have to eat and keep going. Eating is a small, good thing at a time like this ... Eat up. Eat all you want"—what do we have but a kind of communion, a holy meal in which forgiveness transforms former enemies into kindred? Alienated souls who can, in the wee hours of the morning, break bread together and not think of leaving?

It may be enough to say that Carver rethought an earlier story of lost souls hopelessly cut off from one another so that it could become instead a story of hope. No doubt his experience in Alcoholics Anonymous, with its reliance on a Higher Power and the grace of community, had a great deal to do with this transformation. We Christians have much to learn from the Twelve Step movement about acceptance as the prelude to change. We also need to keep in mind Esau's tearful embrace of Jacob as well as the priorities of the Prodigal's father, who knew that what finally mattered was that the one thought dead was in fact alive, the one who was lost, found.

And then there is the revelation closer at hand. Among the many blessings of Frank Griswold's ministry, and especially during his years as Presiding Bishop, has been his willingness to stay at the table, to keep talking even into the wee hours—to keep breaking bread with anyone who will taste and see. As the baker says, "You have to eat and keep going. Eating is a small, good thing at a time like this ... Eat up. Eat all you want." It takes courage to look hatred in the face and not pull away, to persist against the odds. It also takes humility to acknowledge that the good things one can actually accomplish may be very small indeed. Yet no one can miss the graced occasion when it comes, whether at a baker's wooden table or a cathedral's high altar. "How good and pleasant it is when kindred live together in unity!" How rare, but how good.

Notes

1. Raymond Carver, "The Bath," *What We Talk About When We Talk About Love* (New York: Random House, 1981), 48.

2. Ibid., 49.

3. Ibid., 56.

4. Raymond Carver, "A Small, Good Thing," *Cathedral* (New York: Random House, 1984), 60.

5. Ibid., 83.

6. Ibid.

7. Ibid., 86–87.

8. Ibid., 87–88.

9. Ibid., 60.

10. Ibid., 89.

Sacramental Aspects of Reconciliation: Impaired Communion and Eschatological Hope

Louis Weil

RECONCILIATION has been the central message of the primacy of Frank Griswold, whose ministry we celebrate and honor here. Reconciliation is the message at the heart of the gospel and was a fundamental aspect of St. Paul's preaching. In his second letter to the Christians at Corinth the imperative sounds quite clearly:

> If anyone is in Christ, he is a new creation; the old has passed away, behold, the new has come. All this is from God, who through Christ reconciled us to himself and gave us the ministry of reconciliation; that is, God was in Christ reconciling the world to himself, not counting their trespasses against them, and entrusting to us the message of reconciliation. So we are ambassadors for Christ, God making his appeal through us. We beseech you on behalf of Christ, be reconciled to God.[1]

Here we see the two dimensions of the imperative of reconciliation: our redemption through Christ ends our alienation from God and also compels us toward reconciliation with our fellow human beings. Jesus identified himself in the most radical way with those we encounter in our daily lives: the hungry, the thirsty, the naked, the sick, and those in prison, saying that "as you did it to one of the least of these, you did it to me."[2] Thus, we cannot claim that we are reconciled to God if we live in alienation from our brothers and sisters.

This mutuality between God's love for us and our love for others is further confirmed in the First Letter of John:

> We love because he first loved us. If anyone says, "I love God," and hates his brother, he is a liar; for he who does not love his brother whom he has seen, cannot love God whom he has not seen. And this commandment we have from him, that he who loves God should love his brother also.[3]

The widely inclusive imperative of reconciliation central to the New Testament requires of us the often-difficult work of reconciliation with our fellow creatures, even those with whom we find ourselves in conflict.

Conflict is not new to the church; we find evidence of conflict stretching back even to the lives of the apostles. One need only point to the bitter struggles over the circumcision of Gentile converts[4] or the disagreement between Paul and Barnabas.[5] The history of conflict within the church from the very beginning, and the reality of the all-too-human condition of alienation, makes Paul's appeal for reconciliation all the more urgent. As the Dominican ecumenist J.-M. R. Tillard has commented:

> Except perhaps for the texts linked to the tradition of Pentecost, it is remarkable that the major documents in Scripture concerning ecclesial *koinonia* (in the global sense of the word) are in one way or another conditioned by tense situations, perhaps even by conflicts which are able to lead to splits or divisions. The clay vessels which contain the treasure are not only individuals but also communities. Besides, the history of the church can be viewed . . . as marked by splits . . . which always leave their mark. We have examples dating from the frictions of the Greeks and the Hebrews, the conflicts between disciples of James and Christians who had come over from paganism, and the tensions between the Johannine communities and others. *Communion* does not shine forth in all its splendor except on too few occasions, even if the obstacles that are perceived in the New Testament do not necessarily indicate a break or separation. Rarely has communion been realized in its perfection on the universal plane.[6]

Though conflict has been a constant factor in the church's life, it is also true that within the Anglican tradition a way has been found to contain conflicting views within a context of common prayer. From the time the Church of England separated from papal authority in the sixteenth century, Anglican history has been marked by what we might call Catholic and Protestant polarities. In these polarities we plainly see the tension between quite disparate understandings of the interpretation of Scripture and of Christian doctrine.

In the sixteenth century Queen Elizabeth I hoped to establish a Catholic church of the English people which would contain those polarities and whose cohesion would be supported by a broad religious consensus. This national church would embrace fundamentals from the heritage of Western Catholicism and the principal theological concerns of the Reformers, including the rejection of papal authority. Elizabeth was never able fully to achieve that goal. The Puritan movement within the national church soon demanded reforms that eventually pushed it into separation, while the commitment of the Catholic wing to the papacy made of Roman Catholicism an underground church that continued to arouse suspicions both political and religious. However, through what is known as the Elizabethan settlement, Queen Elizabeth did establish a national church that, by espousing a principle of toleration of diversity in both faith and practice, was able to include in its fold the majority of the English people.

This mutual toleration meant that Christians in England who found themselves at very different points on the Catholic–Protestant spectrum were, at least in principle, united in Eucharistic communion. Thus, people of different theological views were *reconciled;* their theological conflict did not undermine sacramental unity.

And that brings us to this present day and the concept of "impaired communion" that has arisen recently within the Anglican Communion. I would assert that giving credence to this notion represents a serious erosion of the principle that our unity in the Body of Christ has greater significance than doctrinal conflict. This is because reconciliation is directly related to the unity of the church that we profess as an article of faith in the Nicene Creed.

Unity and Communion

If unity is a "mark" of the church's essential nature, a mark that has, as Tillard says, rarely been perfectly realized, how are we to understand the unity that we profess each time we say the Creed? In order to attempt to answer this question, we must look at the sacramental dimension of the church's life. For Anglicans, the link between the imperative of reconciliation and the sacramental life of the church is most clearly expressed in the confession of sins, either as a corporate confession during a liturgy or a private confession made to a priest. Yet these two forms are not the fulfillment of what the church has understood as the sacramental aspect of reconciliation. That fulfillment is found always in the Eucharist, which is the great act of reconciliation in the sacramental life of the church. Rites of reconciliation, whether corporate or private, are always ordered toward the reconciliation embodied in the Eucharist. In the sharing of the Eucharistic gifts all the threads of the church's life come together and the restored baptismal dignity that reconciliation effects finds full expression.

Our liturgical rites, particularly the sacraments of Baptism and Eucharist, have a great deal to say to us about the unity of the church. First, I would affirm that these two sacraments are the primary liturgical embodiment of the prayer of Christ for his disciples, and thus for the church, *ut unum sint,* "that they may all be one."[7] With regard to baptism, this affirmation emerges from a baptismal ecclesiology, that is, from a defining of the unity of the church as grounded in the identity shared by all baptized Christians: the church as the Body of Christ. With regard to the Eucharist, my affirmation rests upon the role of the Holy Spirit in every proclamation of the Great Prayer of Thanksgiving, which is the heart of the Eucharistic action. I see this work of the Spirit as an essential expression of the unity which baptism effects. In the Eucharistic Prayer, the Spirit's activity has been generally understood as ordered toward the unity of Christians both through the Spirit's agency in the consecration of the Gifts, and through the people's sharing of those Gifts, the sacramental Body and Blood of the Lord, as the outward sign of their common faith.[8] I would suggest that our divisions and our tendency toward conflict are a clear sign that the unity we profess in the Creed is not yet realized; it is, rather, a future hope, what theologians would call "an eschatological hope." What would be the effect of considering these sacramental acts within an eschatological perspective? How might we come to see unity *not* as an idealized norm from the past that has in fact been shattered throughout much of the church's history? Might we see this unity rather as a promise of the future fulfillment toward which Baptism and Eucharist orient the church?

Baptismal Ecclesiology and Disunity

In the ecumenical dialogues between the various Christian traditions, agreements on Baptism and Eucharist have been generally easy to achieve. The truly divisive issues have tended to cluster around the diverse models of ordained leadership in the various traditions and the closely related issue of ministerial authority.[9] From what was said earlier, it seems that the significant agreement on the theologies of Baptism and Eucharist which has been achieved in the various ecumenical documents offers a basis upon which a greater degree of unity might be realized. There is a painful irony in the fact that at a time when ecumenical dialogues have moved our various ecclesial communities toward the sharing of the Eucharistic gifts, we find within each tradition polarizations that undermine unity in the Eucharist. The issue of "impaired communion" is not a problem only for Anglicans.

Behind this situation there lies the familiar presupposition that Christians should not share communion until all disputed questions have been reconciled. In the past, this has been a question between different traditions, but it has now appeared among Christians of the same church. In this view, intercommunion is possible only when disagreements regarding faith and practice have been resolved. Communion thus becomes the sign of a unity *already achieved.* This view was stated in the Report of the Fourth World Conference on Faith and Order in these words:

> Some Christians believe that eucharistic communion, being an expression of the acceptance of the whole Christ, implies full unity in the wholeness of his truth; that there cannot be any "intercommunion" between otherwise separated Christians; that communion in the sacraments therefore implies a pattern of doctrine and

ministry which is indivisible; and that "inter-communion" cannot presume upon the union in faith that we still seek.[10]

Given the reality of institutional divisions which have been characteristic of the church for at least a millennium (if we think first of the Great Schism between East and West in 1054), but which can be found on a lesser scale throughout the church's history, it was inevitable that conflict would affect the sharing of Eucharistic communion. In that context, intercommunion was inconceivable without the complete resolution of all the issues that divided the respective ecclesial bodies. The unity created by the one baptism was undermined by the impact of a schismatic spirit. But now we find this view *within* what has been known as a single ecclesial body.

Within the context of a baptismal ecclesiology, however, differences in doctrine would not be seen as the defining characteristics separating one group from another, but rather as differences *within* the one Body which includes all the baptized. In other words, a baptismal ecclesiology rests upon the foundation we find in St. Paul's letter to the Ephesians: "There is one body, and one Spirit . . . one Lord, one faith, one baptism, one God and Father of us all, who is above all and through all and in all."[11] The vision presented here is one that would embrace differences among Christians as inviting dialogue and the sharing of faith experience, and as a summons to a higher commitment of unity in Christ, a unity which is not menaced by diversity in faith and practice. In the face of the present crisis in Anglicanism, this seems naïvely optimistic, but it does take seriously the unity which baptism effects. This is the view that was put forth at the same Conference on Faith and Order in these words:

> Some Christians believe that the degree of ecclesial communion which we have in the body of Christ, through baptism and through our fundamental faith, although we are still divided on some points, urges us to celebrate Holy Communion together and to promote intercommunion between the churches. It is Christ, present in the Eucharist, who invites all Christians to his table: this direct invitation of Christ cannot be thwarted by ecclesiastical discipline. In the communion at the same holy table, divided Christians are committed in a decisive way to make manifest their total, visible and organic unity.[12]

This alternative theological approach to the relation of communion to Christian unity sees the Eucharist as an effective or causative sign of unity, that is, that the Eucharist embodies the grace to *effect* the unity which it signifies. On the whole, this second approach has not received adequate attention. It is, however, a strong expression of the implications of a baptismal ecclesiology. The assumption on which it rests is that baptism creates the unity of the one church, and that although human sin may scar that unity, it cannot annihilate it.

Communion grounded in the one baptism is oriented toward the future. It sees the divisions in the church as real but not ultimate, and is thus oriented toward the hoped-for fulfillment when all of God's people will be gathered in unity around their Lord at the *eschaton*. This second approach is thus clearly eschatological in its orientation.

The recovery of a baptismal ecclesiology will necessarily require a creative engagement with the clerical ecclesiology that has dominated the church's self-understanding for well over a millennium. Although there are authentic values in the heritage of the ecclesiology that has shaped most of us, whether laity or clergy, what is required is a transformation of the church's self-understanding in ways that incorporate the vision of a baptismal ecclesiology.

British theologian Paul Avis has brought helpful insight to these questions. He writes,

> There are many thousands of Christian communions, large and small, in the world. Doubtless each has its own integrity after a fashion and each can appeal to the dominical promise: "Where two or three are gathered together in my name, there I am in the midst." Each must learn to regard the others as genuine expressions, albeit with limitations due to history, theology and other factors, of the mystical Body of Christ. We need to work for greater mutual understanding in the context of total mutual acceptance on the basis of our baptism into Christ and the fundamental Trinitarian baptismal faith of the Church. This can be done, I believe, without sacrificing or compromising what is distinctive and precious in our own tradition. This is the key to finding a new paradigm for Anglicanism, and indeed for ecumenical Christianity.[13]

What Avis calls "a new paradigm" is an ecclesiology that begins from the essential unity of the one church of Jesus Christ into which we have been baptized. Yet the understanding that flows out of mutual acceptance is more easily affirmed than achieved. Mutual acceptance embodied in reconciliation seems particularly elusive at this time. The one church is the church in human history, a community of faith in which human fallibility is a constant factor in the all-too-human tendency toward ideological separation. The Eucharist is not a Band-Aid for a cancer. The integrity of Eucharistic celebrations requires authentic reconciliation, but at the same time, the sharing of the Eucharistic gifts can, as we have observed, help us toward the resolution of conflict through the affirmation that our unity in Christ embodied in the sharing of communion is more binding upon us than disputed questions.

Eschatology and Unity

The decision of the American Church to ordain to the episcopate a partnered gay man, and the decision in the Church of Canada (in the Diocese of New Westminster) to authorize the blessing of same-sex unions, were the presenting events that raised the issue of "impaired communion" for Anglicans.[14] But these issues are, I would suggest, footnotes to the larger questions raised at the beginning of this essay: What is the nature of the unity of the church which is created by baptism and which we profess in the Nicene Creed? How is that unity embodied in the sharing of the Eucharistic gifts? And what would be the impact of placing these questions within an eschatological context?

The English Methodist theologian Geoffrey Wainwright, in his book *Eucharist and Eschatology*, offers a schema of the related issues regarding the Eucharist, Christian unity, and eschatology. He writes that "the eschatological nature of the eucharist compels divided Christians towards the practice of intercommunion."[15] When Christians are divided, Wainwright suggests, there can be no satisfactory doctrinal formulation of the relation between the church and the sacraments: the sacraments are ordered toward unity, not division.

So it is that the fundamental anomaly is our divisions, yet that is the real world in which we live. Because of this profound anomaly, *all* celebrations of the Eucharist in all of the various Christian traditions are in some sense impaired because they point to an ecclesial unity that is not a lived reality for the church in our world. It is important to recognize this larger context for the question of "impaired communion." The whole church lives with impaired communion, yet we are so accustomed to our denominational divisions that we easily forget that this is itself the fundamental anomaly.

We must avoid being myopic about the question of impaired communion *within* the Anglican Communion. This may be forced upon us by fundamentalist, neo-puritan voices who are seeking separation from the "tainted" American and Canadian churches. In saying this, I am by no means suggesting that further schism is desirable. Yet we are more aware today than in past generations how often what we might call "conflicting truths" are grounded in widely divergent cultural contexts. Bridging these divides is a more arduous task than our religious structures have thus far been able to accommodate. The threat of schism is all too real when widely differing cultural "languages" can find no meeting point. We are then left with the problem of differing understandings of truth and with very different approaches as to how the scriptures are to be interpreted.

As we saw earlier, there is a well-established tradition in Christianity that unity in faith (and this would include, it seems, unity in regard to the interpretation of Scripture) must be a prerequisite for the sharing of communion. Where this view is in force, simple honesty must oblige us to admit that significant barriers to the sharing of communion already exist. Schism has taken place in the past, and, sadly, may occur again in the days ahead. Yet our unity in the one baptism establishes our unity in the one church in spite of our sinful divisions.

On the other hand, as we have observed, the sharing of communion in the Eucharist may be looked at not only as the goal at the end of the path to doctrinal agreement, but may also be seen as an effective means toward unity, that the sharing of the Eucharist can help us to realize the unity into which we have been baptized. Wainwright is again helpful in this regard. In his discussion of the contrast between "the Lord's supper and the church's supper," he writes:

> In a state of affairs marred by human sin (and Christian disunity is such a state), we may be obliged to choose between the order Christ-church-sacraments and Christ-sacraments-church. In that case the choice must fall in favour of the second. . . . The need to choose, and then this positive choice, are forced upon us by the fact that human sin may cause a degree of separation between the church and its Lord

(and result in a division among Christians and in faulty performance of the sacraments which the Lord has given His church to perform as signs by which to enjoy and proclaim the kingdom of God) but that the sacraments remain the Lord's entirely, and may be used by Him, even when (at the purely human level) defectively performed, as the vehicles of His presence to bring His church to a more obedient acknowledgement . . . of the kingdom of God. In the light of this eschatological purpose, no obstacle of ecclesiastical discipline dependent on a sinful state of Christian disunity must be allowed to block the Lord's invitation to *all* penitents among His sinning people to gather round His table wherever it is set up and to receive His forgiveness for sins that have led to disunity and be filled through His transforming presence with the love that unites.[16]

In the face of Christian disunity, and the possibility of further division, our divided Christian traditions are obliged to acknowledge the provisional character of all celebrations of the Eucharist. The eschatological nature of the Eucharist suggested here always points us to future fulfillment. Our celebration of the Eucharist here on earth is a foretaste of the heavenly banquet that Scripture holds out to us as a promise of the future when all of God's people will be gathered in unity around Christ in the kingdom of God and where our reconciliation with God and with all the members of God's human family will be complete.

Notes

1. 2 Cor. 5:17–20.

2. Matt. 25:31–46.

3. 1 John 4.

4. Acts 15:1–21; cf. Paul's account in Galatians 2 in which he says, speaking of his disagreement with Peter, "I opposed him to his face."

5. Acts 15:35–41.

6. J.-M. R. Tillard, *Church of Churches: The Ecclesiology of Communion* (Collegeville, Minn.: Liturgical Press, 1992), 33.

7. John 17:11.

8. Cf. my article "Holy Spirit: Source of Unity in the Liturgy" in *Engaging the Spirit,* ed. R. B. Slocum (New York: Church Publishing, 2001), 39–45. Thus we may appropriately speak not only of the Real Presence of Christ in the Eucharist, but also of the Real Presence of the Holy Spirit.

9. Cf. my "Baptismal Ecclesiology: Uncovering a Paradigm." Essay in process of publication among papers commissioned after the IALC meeting at Cuddesdon, Oxford, in 2003.

10. P. C. Rodger and L. Vischer, eds., *Report of the Fourth World Conference on Faith and Order, Montreal 1963* (London: WCC, Faith and Order Paper No. 42), 78, Par. 139.

11. Eph. 4:4–6.

12. Op. cit., Par. 138.

13. *Anglicanism and the Christian Church* (London: T. & T. Clark, 2002), 346.

14. On this issue, cf. my article "Rome and Canterbury—Steps Toward Reconciliation Through the Sharing of Gifts," *Semi-Annual Bulletin,* Centro Pro Unione 67, Rome (Spring 2005): 16–20.

15. *Eucharist and Eschatology* (New York: Oxford University Press, 1981), 137.

16. Loc. cit.

A Friend for the Journey,
A Guide along the Way

Luci Shaw

I MET OUR PRESIDING BISHOP, our "P.B.," before he was internationally famous, though he had recently been installed as Bishop of Chicago, a not insignificant post.

I had recently lost my husband and closest confidant and was working my way through grief. As a writer, immersed in the world of my own words, and thus too close to them to be objective about their worth and how they might embody spiritual verities, I asked my close friend Eugene Peterson for advice. He had been talking to the Chrysostom Society, a group to which we have both belonged for years, about the need a writer has for a spiritual director—one who might be a guide in growing us further, as Christians, into the image of Christ, the great Communicator, the Logos.

"But how," I queried, "do I find this person? Where do I begin to look? And how do I find out if she or he is right for me?" I knew I needed accountability, but I also yearned for compatibility—for someone who understood the importance of literature as a road marker in our culture and an expression of my own Christian spirituality, someone who was a poet at heart.

Eugene was bluff and brief in his answer. "Pray about it," he said. "See whose picture pops into your head."

I did, and was perplexed. "Frank Griswold, Bishop of Chicago?" I wondered to myself. Surely such a busy prelate would have responsibilities far greater than listening to the murmurings of a poet. "Well, ask him," responded Eugene when I mentioned this on the phone. "The worst he can do is say No."

I had already met Frank's wife, Phoebe, over a meal, and called her for advice. "Why don't you and Frank meet for lunch, and see if it's a good fit," she suggested. I made the appointment. We met in downtown Chicago. And it was a good fit. Frank told me, "I'd much rather have conversations with a spiritual seeker than chair any number of diocesan committees!"

And so it was. Depending on his, and my own, busy schedules we met at his office in the Episcopal Church Center in Chicago for nearly three fruitful years.

Frank was a superb listener, and a wise and insightful counselor. Through Ignatian spirituality, he introduced me to an understanding of the personal journey of desolations and consolations, and I began to feel my own quivering faith grow stronger, and to experience an inner reconciliation, a right ordering of heart.

So it is with deep gratitude that I dedicate the three following poems to him, and the blessings of his companionship in a time of loneliness and need: "Sensing," "Crossing," and "Rounding."

Sensing
St. Paul's, Bellingham

A bloom like phosphorescence shines on
the newel posts at the ends of the pews. Is it the
    candles
standing on the altar, fat and white as milk,
with their heads on fire—vowels of light? Is it

the winter sun bleeding through stained glass
so that our faces begin to burn like lanterns?
Is it the air, with its brew of scents: varnished
    wood,
heat from the old radiators, and a whiff of
    consecrated oil?

There's the salt of old sweat, a profligacy of
    spice—
pungent distress and quandary and creed.
The seed of faith being sown again and again,
the fragrance of psalms, and their ancient verbal
    music.

The brassy cross in procession, an organ
    flourish,
and kneelers that creak when we slump down,
    confessing.
Gospel words from the aisle and the pulpit, the
    tread
of steps up to the altar, shriven souls inhaling,

hands and lips lifted for food and drink, the
    giving and taking

of ourselves—the commerce of heaven. Perhaps
    it's a kind
of incense just to be this—the prosaic body of
    God with peace
and grace passed among us, and a few crimson
    choir robes.

Crossing

My right hand—
when I cross myself—
patterns me with Presence
—Father, Son,
and Holy Ghost—
here in my head, my heart
(where I need it most),
my left side and my right.
Thus crossed before the cross,
I am signed both with
death and life,
the intersection of
darkness with light.

 But with that crossing
in whatever holy place,
my dexterous right hallows
its sinister fellow.
Through Grace
rather than competing,
the agile blesses
the awkward part,
the strong (the one

that feeds me when I'm eating)
exalts the weak.

At Eucharist, or at table
for any sustaining meal,
the food I manage with
my right hand also feeds
the part less able
on its own to spoon, or speak
for its own needs.
So, here I kneel,
left hand cupped under right,
taking for both enough bread
for the journey,
for each, enough strength
for the week.

Rounding

I ask each of the icons above my desk
a personal question—That nimbus around
your solemn head, is it a burden?
Or is its gold beaten air-thin, a wisp of wafer
like the round leaf of fiber floated onto our
    tongues
at the altar? A circle—in a wedding ring
it speaks for a union without flaw. How can this
    ring
be mended if it gets worn, lost, broken?
And the moon, fat as a pearl, a grape, a wheel
of cheese—in two weeks gnawed away a bit
    more

every night, like a wheat cracker, by
the mice of heaven, by what mystery is it fleshed
    out
to roundness like the planets, the suns?

At Eucharist the priest holds high, in his thin
hands, a disc almost as big as a dinner plate.
He bends this little sun vertically in half
and half again; it cracks each time with a sound
that splits the sanctuary like an arrow, and us
with it. So, we take this broken Son onto
our tongues. Swallowed, into our gut. Eating,
we join bodily the whole holy Circle of God.

The Concept of Paradox:
A Paradigm of Reconciliation

J. Robert Wright

E PISCOPALIANS ARE ALREADY familiar with the concept of "paradox" from the Historical Documents section of the Book of Common Prayer, as indeed anyone should be who studies the history of the early church and its doctrine, whereby the Episcopal Church affirms that Jesus is both divine and human and that God is both three and one. The former paradox is the central affirmation of the Chalcedonian Definition of Faith (451 CE) and the latter paradox is found in the teaching of the creed commonly called that of Saint Athanasius.[1] These two great paradoxes of patristic doctrine enabled reconciliation to occur and diverging views of God and Christ to co-exist in agreed formulas within the history and doctrine of the early church. But how does the concept of "paradox" play out in the writing and teaching of one who has been so prominent a church leader in our own day? In salutation to the Presiding Bishop and Primate, this present essay will trace the theme of "paradox" in the writings, sermons, and addresses of Frank T. Griswold that are dated and published and made openly available on the Episcopal

Church's official website.[2] It is my contention that this concept has been quite central to his thought and leadership, and that he has often, almost regularly, used it as a way of mentally and verbally dealing with difficulties that at first seem irreconcilable or insurmountable. In fact, I believe it is a key to understanding the theological thought that underlies his style of leadership and his attempt to offer a paradigm of reconciliation for the church of our time. This essay will focus upon the words he has published on this theme, with a concluding personal evaluation at the end.

I first became aware of how very central the concept of paradox is in the thought of Frank Griswold when I heard the sermon he preached at his investiture as the twenty-fifth Presiding Bishop in Washington National Cathedral on January 10, 1998. There he remarked, in what would become a typical frame of reference for him, that "a capacity for ambiguity and paradox is part of the glory and frustration of the Anglican way. Richard Hooker, possibly the greatest theologian in the history of Anglicanism, observed . . . that though we long for 'the most infallible certainty which the nature of things can yield,' we proceed, in actual fact, by way of 'probable persuasions.'" "The Anglican tradition," the new Primate continued, "because of its 'graced pragmatism'—its reasonableness formed by Scripture and Tradition—possesses a unique capacity for diversity, and the ability to discern and welcome truth in its various forms. Through the subtle yet exacting rhythms of our common prayer, the diverse and the disparate, the contradictory and the paradoxical are woven together in the risen Christ through the ever unfolding and always challenging mystery of communion." Next, he exclaimed proleptically, "What we as the Episcopal Church shall be as we look to the future has yet to be revealed." And then, in another turn of speech that would become typical, he reinforced his point by a brief reference to one of the writers of the early church, St. Isaac of Nineveh from the seventh century, an admonition that we need "a purified and transformed heart" which, "in more contemporary terms, is open to the paradoxes and contradictions of life."[3]

Here, therefore, at the very outset of his primatial ministry, the new Presiding Bishop had given a major insight as to how he would understand and utilize the concept of "paradox." "By paradox," he defined in another address, "I mean the capacity to embrace seemingly irreconcilable opposites as part of one truth." The reality of paradox, he explained at the same time, means "moving from a perspective of either/or to one of both/and."[4] Upon his return from the Lambeth Conference of 1998, he spoke to the same theme: "All contradictions and paradoxes and seemingly irreconcilable truths—which seem both consistent and inconsistent with Scripture— are brought together in the larger and all-embracing truth of Christ, which, by Christ's own words, has yet to be fully drawn forth and known."[5] Often, he would subsequently add, it is only through paradox and contradiction "that the divine compassion breaks into our lives," for "paradox and contradiction are part of the very mystery of creation itself."[6] In such fundamental statements Bishop Griswold was also giving hints as to how he would develop this theme with reference to two other words and two other phrases that are closely related but subordinate to his thought on paradox: the words "ambiguity" and "contradiction," and the phrases "seeming irreconcilability" and "unfolding truth." At times he comes close to using all these as synonyms, but as one travels through his published writings it becomes apparent that he uses these related words and phrases only in subordination to "paradox," and that "paradox" itself is the dominant concept that he follows in these contexts.

Less than three years after his investiture in Washington Cathedral, in his remarks for the orientation of bishops and deputies at the opening of the 73rd General Convention, the Presiding Bishop drew very directly upon the frameworks of paradox embedded in the affirmations of the early church that have already been mentioned at the opening of this essay. In remarks that were clearly anchored in patristic foundations, he said: "The tradition of the church has shown us that a capacity for paradox is integral to orthodoxy and has been with us since the beginning. Take for example the doctrine of the Trinity in which we contemplate the mystery of God who is both three and one—not three *or* one. 'The divine is indivisible in its divisions,' observed Gregory of Nazianzus in the fourth century. 'Both the distinction and the union alike are paradoxical.' Or again, the Chalcedonian definition printed in our Prayer Book, dated 451, in which the divine and human natures of Christ are declared coexistent without confusion or separation. Christ therefore is not either human or divine as the early Christological heresies argued, but rather both human and divine. As we see, paradox in the life of the church is not a contemporary construction."[7] In this way, the Primate embellished the patristic foundations with modern applications. Let us now travel through more of the Presiding Bishop's published thoughts on this concept, citing his own words and constructing a simultaneous mosaic on the subject, before we conclude with a brief personal evaluation.

Paradox, for Frank Griswold, permeates the whole of life in such a way that not only are there individual paradoxes but also, to him, "reality as it is actually lived is largely complex, ambiguous and paradoxical."[8] This understanding even extends to the very person of God, who is "lovingly paradoxical, ambiguous, playful, ironic."[9] Even God's ways, unfathomable and mysterious, are filled with contradiction, ambiguity, and paradox.[10] Likewise truth itself is paradoxical, for there are "many and sometimes seemingly contradictory ways in which the Spirit of truth seeks always to lead us into Christ's ever-unfolding truth."[11] Indeed, "my thoughts are not your thoughts nor your ways my ways" is a Scripture verse he often cites in support.[12] Other important examples of "paradox" as they appear in the Presiding Bishop's writings include: becoming foolish in order to become wise, relinquishing in order to possess,[13] and, especially, finding or gaining one's life by losing it for the sake of the Gospel.[14] The latter he describes as a teaching in which Jesus spoke out of the personal experience of his own struggle to discern the will of the One who had sent him.[15] All this is why, in baptism, there is a "paradoxical pattern of dying and rising, losing and finding, becoming strong by encountering weakness, being made rich by experiencing our existential poverty."[16] Another example is the paradox of Jesus leaving the apostles by way of the Ascension, which was really a way by which they came to know him more closely.[17] Another is the way in which Christ's power is paradoxically realized in the midst of our own weakness and inadequacy.[18] Likewise, the paradox of an aging body is balanced by interior strength, the paradox of suffering balanced by the glorious liberty of the children of God.[19] In fact, if a person takes the losses in one's life up into Christ, then "instead of being diminished by them," . . . "paradoxically one is increased by them."[20] In still another context of paradox or ambiguity, while discussing human sexuality, he quotes the poet William Blake in an poem written in 1818: "Both read the Bible day and night, But thou readest black where I read white."[21] The truth may unfold, however, in such a way that what seems certain to one person may seem uncertain to another, and so it is that we should cultivate the ability to "enter into another's truth, another's joys and burdens, another's ambiguities and paradoxes."[22]

Such advice goes only so far, of course, in the current debates about human sexuality, for what seems to be the truth in one part of the world, or at least to the majority of those living in that part of it, or to the majority of those voting in one small church in one part of it, or to those living at one chronological point in the historical continuum, may well not be the case for the majority of those living in another part of the world or in another church in another part of it, or at another point in time. In a letter to the Editor of the *New York Times* Bishop Griswold had already pointed out in 1998 that "The context in which one church or province of the Anglican Communion seeks to interpret and live the gospel may be very different from the context and application of that same gospel in another province. What appears to be good news in one culture may be perceived to be bad news elsewhere." He added, though: "This is not to suggest that a particular culture determines the truth of the Christian message."[23] Thus, the

Presiding Bishop evidently believes that there is but one truth, albeit differently perceived in different locales at different times by different people, but he also reminds us of the paradox that God's truth is never static but always unfolding. A sermon he delivered in Honolulu Cathedral in December 2004 began with the obvious yet profound observation that "God's mysterious ways draw us beyond certitude into an ever unfolding truth which has its beginning and end, its alpha and omega, in the person of Christ who is himself the truth," but the sermon then went on to urge that "Christ, however, doesn't simply *tell* the truth or *teach* the truth. He *is* the truth, a truth which can only be entered into and known relationally and through companionship."[24] We must learn to do this in a corporate context, Bishop Griswold adds, such as in the church or at least in company with others, for "truth is discovered in communion," and for him instances of disagreement over differing perceptions of truth are particular instances when paradox must be welcomed, when we can move beyond simply winning or losing, from a situation of "either/or" to a situation of "both/and." For him this is not just an opportunity for growth in emotional maturity but a matter involving Scripture and doctrine, "integral to genuine orthodoxy and catholicity."[25] Obviously a solution of "both/and" can enable reconciliation to occur, whereas a solution of "either/or" declares that one side has won and the other has lost.

Addressing a word to the Episcopal Church a few months after the confirmation and consecration of Gene Robinson, he expounded further on the same point: "God's truth is ever unfolding and the Holy Spirit is still leading us on. According to Jesus' words in the

Gospel of John it is the function of the Spirit of Truth to lead us ever more deeply into the fullness of truth. Jesus is speaking to his disciples not individually but collectively as a community. He tells them he has many more things to say which they are unable to bear at the present moment. He tells them the Spirit will draw from what is his and make it known to them. From this we know," the Primate concluded, "that the appropriation of 'the truth as in Jesus' is a process of continuing prayer and discernment which involves us both personally and collectively as a community of faith."[26] Even Mary's response to the Annunciation, Bishop Griswold says in another context, can be seen as her "progressive and ever unfolding 'yes'" to God's truth that was being revealed to her.[27] Similarly, for the feast of St. Anselm in 1998, and elsewhere, he made reference to "the developmental nature of grace mediated by the circumstances of our lives and the agency of the Holy Spirit."[28]

For Bishop Griswold, the concept of unfolding truth is close to but always subordinate under the concept of paradox, and it is derived primarily from John 8:31–32 ("You will know the truth and the truth will make you free") and John 16:12–14 ("I still have many things to say to you but you cannot bear them now. When the Spirit of truth comes, he will guide you into all the truth. . . . He will take what is mine and declare it to you").[29] Although not every paradox necessarily leads to an unfolding truth, I think he would say, yet it is also true that new paradoxes as well as unfolding truth can be further generated from these scriptural foundations, as he early intimated in the essay he wrote on "Anglican Spirituality" around the time of the Lambeth Conference of 1998: "The fact that Jesus had more to 'say' to his disciples than they could presently bear or assimilate (John 16:12) makes it clear that God's word in Christ continues to 'go forth' in its ever creative potentiality, and to reveal new meaning and to speak to new situations in our lives personally and as communities of faith with our distinctive cultures, histories, and challenges."[30] Most recently, in two messages dating from around the time of Pentecost 2005, he stated: "It is through the agency of the Holy Spirit that God's creative activity continues in the world and Christ continues to unfold his truth." Developing his message around John 16 he then asked: "Is it not possible that some of the disagreements within the life of the church are part of the Spirit's unrelenting activity in leading us to new and deeper understandings of things we have previously regarded as fully known?"[31]

All these are strong words, of course, demanding concentrated thought, and one underlying question we may wonder is to ask who (in addition to Jesus!) can cope with all of this complicated talk about "paradox" and "unfolding truth"? Bishop Griswold would no doubt cite many who share his own understanding of "paradox" along similar lines, but it is interesting that the one church leader whom he does mention by name in this context is Rowan Williams. Following the Primates' Meeting at Canterbury in April 2002, Bishop Griswold declared, "Obviously the Archbishop of Canterbury has to be someone who can deal with complexity and paradox."[32]

Concluding Personal Evaluation

The legacy of the protestant reformation must lie heavily upon the heart and mind of every Anglican primate whether it be Rowan of Canterbury, or Frank of the USA, or Peter of All Nigeria; and it may serve well in conclusion to bring into the dialogue the now-distant voice of Thomas Cranmer, who in the context of the biblical interpretation of his day stated as follows: "If there were any word of God beside the scripture, we could never be certain of God's word; and if we be uncertain of God's word, the devil might bring in among us a new word, a new doctrine, a new faith, a new church, a new god, yea, himself to be god.... If the church and the Christian faith did not stay itself upon the Word of God certain, as upon a sure and strong foundation, no man could know whether he had a right faith, and whether he were in the true church of Christ, or in the synagogue of Satan."[33] Such axioms were commonplace to the reformers in an age that prized the literal inerrancy of the scriptures that had recently been set in print, and such axioms are still prized today among those who take a fundamentalistic approach to Scripture. The question the Anglican Communion is currently struggling with is precisely how to decide which interpretation of Scripture is the right one, or whether there can be a paradox that facilitates a "both/and" solution, a reconciliation, especially in the face of contradictory interpretations and in the absence of belief in a pope who might be infallible, or of any other final human authority that all sides can recognize.[34]

The contention of this essay has been that the concept of "paradox" is a key that unlocks the thought-process and methodology by which Frank Griswold as Primate has been able to face and deal with contradictions and novelties in the history of the church during his tenure and to offer a template for reconciliation.

Each side of the current divisions over human sexuality, conservative or liberal, may be tempted to claim that this Presiding Bishop has, by his use of the concept of "paradox," sold out to the other side, the conservatives by claiming that he has opted for an open-ended "both/ and" revelation that knows no bounds as it continually unfolds, the liberals by claiming that he has failed to apply his "both/and" paradoxical solution and its related concept of unfolding truth to a specific endorsement of same-sex unions. Neither charge, I believe, will stick, because in his use of such terms, at least in his published writing, he has avoided drawing a conclusion that would allow either side to claim an exclusive victory, with him firmly planted in their own corner. Each side might be tempted to protest that this concept of paradox as he uses it tends to minimize what is at stake for them in the polarity, but this is not possible because he does not name what is at stake when he uses such concepts. He does not actually apply his concept of paradox in specific proposals for reconciliation in particular cases, but rather he states the general principle and leaves others to apply it.

It now seems appropriate to return to Archbishop Cranmer and to conclude by asking, in this context, whether the Presiding Bishop, on the basis of what he has spoken and written and published about "paradox" and "unfolding truth," would see himself as having deviated from the foregoing principle of scriptural interpretation that was set by Archbishop Cranmer centuries ago. My answer is that I doubt he would see himself as having done that, because the scriptural text itself, especially in the Gospel of John, establishes our belief in a living Lord who not merely *wrote* about truth, told it and taught about it, but who *was and is the truth*. And this, I believe Frank would say, is the ultimate paradox that enables the Christian faith to deal with, even to absorb, apparently irreconcilable contradictions and developments.

Notes

1. For both texts, see BCP pp. 864–65.

2. On the web, see www.EpiscopalChurch.org/Presiding Bishop. The postings by year are listed in the left-hand column and will be footnoted in this essay by date of delivery as given. I thank my student Ben Thomas for assistance with online research. Not all of Bishop Griswold's public output is posted here, as will be shown below.

3. January 10, 1998.

4. July 4, 2000.

5. September 1, 1998.

6. August 1, 2003.

7. July 4, 2000.

8. November 17, 2004.

9. November 14, 2004.

10. October 27, 2002; March 28, 1998.

11. November 17, 2004.

12. December 8, 2002.

13. March 28, 1998.

14. September 30, 1998; July 7, 2001; November 14, 2004; February 22, 2005.

15. March 1, 1999.

16. July 1, 2001.

17. May 21, 1998.

18. June 1, 2000; June 1, 2001.

19. January 8, 2005.

20. January 21, 2001.

21. July 4, 2000.

22. July 7, 2000.

23. Undated letter, around the fall of 1998, posted on the Episcopal Church website.

24. December 5, 2004.

25. August 1, 2000.

26. January 22, 2004.

27. March 28, 1998.

28. "Sermon for the Feast of St. Anselm of Canterbury," delivered in the Chapel of the Good Shepherd, General Theological Seminary, April 21, 1998, the text of which is not given on the Episcopal Church's website but printed in *The Anglican* 27, no. 3 (July 1998): 23–25, at 23. Another instance of this term is found in his essay on "Anglican Spirituality," published in *The Essential Guide for the Anglican Communion* by Morehouse Communications for the Anglican Communion Office, London, around the time of the 1998 Lambeth Conference, the text of which is posted on the Episcopal Church's website.

29. December 1, 1998; September 30, 1998; May 1, 1998; July 4, 2000; August 1, 2000.

30. Undated essay published in *The Essential Guide for the Anglican Communion* by Morehouse Communications for the Anglican Communion Office, London, around the time of the 1998 Lambeth Conference, the text of which is posted on the Episcopal Church's website.

31. May 1, 2005; May 13, 2005.

32. May 3, 2002.

33. *The Works of Thomas Cranmer, Archbishop of Canterbury, Martyr, 1556,* ed. John Edmund Cox. Vol. II, *Miscellaneus Writings and Letters of Thomas Cranmer, Archbishop of Canterbury.* Parker Society (Cambridge: Cambridge University Press, 1846, reprint 1968), p. 52.

34. See *The Windsor Report,* whose text is posted on the Anglican Communion website (www.AnglicanCommunion.org) and papers written about it posted upon the General Seminary website (www.GTS.edu) as well as in the recent issue of the *Anglican Theological Review.*

Truth and Unity—
Justice and Reconciliation

Njongonkulu Ndungane

A BISHOP'S LIFE encompasses a great deal—and a primate's is particularly full.

Two elements at the heart of this calling are the provision of a focus of unity in the life of God's people and their mission in the world, and the task of teaching and interpreting the truth as it is in Christ Jesus. Within the ordinal, these form part of what is to be a comprehensive and coherent pattern for episcopal life. Within contemporary life, it often appears that truth and unity are rather more in competition.

In paying tribute to Frank Griswold, and his time as Presiding Bishop, I want to reflect on the tensions of leadership in the church that so often arise in this area. But I shall do so by looking through the prism of two other concepts—justice and reconciliation. These, for me, convey a dynamic outworking of what might otherwise be static and abstract notions.

Our God is a living and active Lord, and his nature is reflected in his self-revelation. Our unity with him, and with each other, comes through his reconciling outreach to his creation. Truthfulness, especially in the Hebrew Scriptures, finds expression through the conforming of our lives, of our world, to the standards of God's righteousness. "Just and true are your ways" is Revelation's Song of the Lamb.[1] And so all God's people are called to pursue justice,[2] and to share in his ministry of reconciliation.[3]

Upholding truth and unity is often a difficult calling, and a serious test of leadership. Yet no matter how impossible it may seem at times, avoiding it is not an option. So in paying tribute to Frank Griswold, for whom both justice and reconciliation are longstanding passions, I want to reflect on the challenges these bring in a broken and fragmented world.

Let me begin with the unity that is found hand in hand with the diversity of the one God, who is Father, Son, and Holy Spirit. God the Father, through his Son, by the power of the Holy Spirit, has been pleased to draw us into this mystical dance of three Persons in one Being, by reconciling to himself all things, all of creation. And he is also pleased to draw all his children to share in that ongoing work of reconciliation, that brings with it righteousness of life and justice in all our dealings—the "repair of the world," or *tikkun-olam,* as Frank reminds us it is known to our Jewish brothers and sisters.[4]

This is no light task. It cost the Son of God his life. From us it demands commitment, determination, effort, and perseverance. It is spiritual warfare in which we are engaged—"waging reconciliation" for the sake of the whole world, as the House of Bishops of the Episcopal Church of the USA (ECUSA) so graphically put it after the terrible events of 9/11.[5]

Three years ago it was a great joy for me to participate, alongside Jeffrey Sachs, in *The Presiding Bishop's*

Forum on Global Reconciliation at the 2003 General Convention. It was a marvelous evening, and through it Frank challenged us all to broaden our understanding of God's reconciliation and to let it bring us "into collaboration and deeper solidarity, in concrete terms that involve us all." We cannot pray for God's kingdom to come, and be indifferent to pain and suffering, injustice and unrighteousness, wherever it is found.

Christians should be at the forefront of the fight against poverty, which, in all its ramifications and consequences, is nothing short of evil. It mars the image of God within humanity; it mars his image in the poor as it deprives them of opportunities for abundant life; and it mars his image within those of us who have more than enough, but who, through greed, complacency, or even ignorance, fail to do the justice, to embrace the loving-kindness, that our God asks of us. Poverty is the new global apartheid.

Yet, even when I look at the terrible statistics, and the human suffering on my own continent of Africa, I am optimistic. I am optimistic about the direction of international relations, and I am optimistic about the ability of the church, working with other faith communities and civil society, to make a reconciling difference.

The Jubilee 2000 campaign gave us our first glimpse of how effectively people-power could move politicians. It was an unprecedented coalition, encompassing the globe, which called for the abolition of odious debt. Politicians were left in no doubt that public opinion, domestic and international, demanded justice in relation to debt. Great steps were taken, and more followed, though we are still not at the end of our journey.

Now politicians need to be left in no doubt that

public opinion, domestic and international, demands justice in relation to poverty and hunger. So we are building on that precedent, even as global leaders also have been turning their gaze to the world's poorest.

The Millennium Development Goals, the Commission for Africa and the G8 Summit, the World Trade Organization's Doha Round—all are rooted in political commitments to make an irreversible improvement to the lives of billions. Alongside this, recipient governments, such as those of the African Union, are also pledging to improve governance so that development programs, whether in aid, trade, or debt forgiveness, can have maximum impact among the most needy.

Now we need to make the politicians keep their promises. The best way to generate the pressure for this is to bring together broad, and vocal, coalitions of voters from across the globe—and there is no one better placed to build such comprehensive networks than the faith communities.

This was evident in June of 2005 when the Presiding Bishop and I, and representatives from over forty faith groups, participated in a "Hunger No More" Convocation at Washington National Cathedral, and called for an end to the injustice of hunger, not just in the poor countries of the world, but also in the huge economic disparities of the richest nation of the planet.

Every major faith group was represented, and Christians of every type imaginable—if only Christian unity were this easy! There is a lesson to learn that when we focus too much on ourselves, and talk about doctrine and the abstract concepts of faith, we find far too many reasons to disagree. But when we put our faith into practice, look what we can achieve together. As it says in the letter of James—faith without works is dead. To quote from Frank Griswold:

> God sent his son to save the world, not the church. The church exists for one purpose and one purpose alone: to embody and to extend the reconciling and boundary-crossing love of God which is the fundamental energy that gives life to the world and is the still point in which everything lives and moves and has its being.[6]

It always amazes me when some Christians speak as if preaching eternal salvation were somehow separable from, and superior to, the bringing of justice to the world around. Both must go hand in hand—each complements the other, for reconciliation with God brings the extension of his kingdom into every area of our lives, so that even our social, political, and economic relations become governed by kindness and mercy, by generosity and faithfulness, by honesty and self-control. All of creation flourishes best according to the life of the Spirit.

Jesus addresses poverty at the very beginning of his ministry. In the synagogue in Nazareth, he lays out what one could call his manifesto, when he reads from the book of the prophet Isaiah:

> "The Spirit of the Lord is upon me,
> because he as anointed me
> to bring good news to the poor.
> He has sent me to proclaim release to the
> captives
> and recovery of sight to the blind,

to let the oppressed go free,
to proclaim a year of the Lord's favor." (Luke
4:18, 19)

The Bread of Life also fed the hungry and healed the sick. The second person of the Trinity took flesh and in doing so dignified our physical existence with all our bodily needs. "Life in abundance" is not just a promise for the world to come. When we read the Bible, we find that gospel salvation and social justice go hand in hand.

Reconciliation operates in many dimensions. It is the reconciliation of creation to the Creator, and the reconciliation of us, God's creatures. Through this also comes the reconciliation of individuals and communities to ourselves and to one another—both inside and outside the church. Wherever in the world there is openness to reconciliation, the Lord is there, and those who have eyes to see will recognize his Spirit powerfully at work.

In South Africa we have been blessed with remarkable evidence of God's reconciling power at work within human society. Apartheid was one of the most divisive political systems ever devised. Even where people would have been happy to live side by side, it kept communities apart and sowed distrust, even hostility. When political change came, we were so fearful of the potential for a bloodbath—as sworn enemies had to overcome bloodshed, even murder, and work together under democracy. The Truth and Reconciliation Commission (TRC), drawing on principles of restorative justice, made a contribution to the ongoing process of building and rebuilding a new South Africa that was nothing short of miraculous.

Restorative justice is profoundly gospel-shaped. It is a systematic response to conflict or wrongdoing that emphasizes healing the wounds of all parties caught up in the rupture of relations—whether offended against, or offending—while also pursuing whatever makes for greater wholeness in the community.

It is a process that certainly upholds the need for justice, expecting those who have caused injury to take steps to repair it. In the secular world, which is increasingly drawing on this approach, it may run in parallel with other, legal, processes. Yet this happens as an intrinsic part of genuine deep encounter between the concerned parties. All sides must be willing to engage openly and honestly, and be prepared to contribute appropriately to help bring resolution, in ways that may only emerge as this holistic process unfolds. The desired outcome is that everyone involved will become contributing members of a community that grows and shapes itself to minimize the possibility of similar harmful actions finding fertile ground.

The ultimate goal of restorative justice is not merely to heal the breach caused when injury is done, but to use the process of restoration as a steppingstone to a more fruitful life for all. It is far more creative than retributive justice—going well beyond addressing wrongdoing and attempting to restore the status quo ante. Often that goal is not an option—irreversible events may have occurred; or, as in the South African situation, there is no sensible "prior starting point" that can operate as a base. Instead of becoming victims of our past, restorative justice gives us a hope-filled future.

This too is gospel-shaped. Redemption does not return us to the Garden of Eden—rather, it invites us to the New Jerusalem. Rowan Williams has said this about our "wound of knowledge": "We can never un-know our past, with its heady power of free will and its anguished pain of choice misused—but neither can we un-know the triumph of the cross and the joy of redemption. Our restoration is as co-heirs with God's Son, who calls us his friends."[7]

Restorative justice is God-shaped justice. Full reconciliation and healing within South Africa will be a long, challenging process that will take at least a generation. Yet it was by God's reconciling mercy, most powerfully shown in the TRC, that we were able to embark on this journey of hope to a New South Africa that is far better than any we have previously known.

So how much greater should be our optimism, when differences arise among God's people, that by his grace we can overcome even painful division, and be spurred on to fuller expressions of his abundant life in his world! This faith can also help us deal honestly with our distinctiveness and not to pretend to a unity of uniformity.

All that Scripture teaches us about creation resonates with both unity and diversity. We know these give rise to inescapable tensions, which we must face head on. There will inevitably be times when we disagree, and I do not think we have yet fathomed all the dimensions of how we hold together in Christ who binds us to himself. The "bonds of affection" that hold our church together are both human-flawed and God-graced. Our human frailties in relationships are interwoven with transcendent possibilities of reconciliation and forgiveness.

Lasting discord and separation can never be God's plan for us—rather, as Paul tells the Corinthians when they dealt with the aftermath of rift, "Satan must not be allowed to get the better of us; we know his wiles all too well." On whatever side of dividing lines brothers and sisters in Christ find ourselves, our greater task is to fight together against the evils of the world, and declare together the greater gospel truths.

Within the church, within the Anglican Communion, we have barely begun to grasp what a process of restorative justice might mean. It has a mutuality and reciprocity in striving together to find the Life-giving Way forward of the one who is the Truth, that is not present in concepts of "restorative discipline" that have been aired.

In these times, the role of Bishop as focus of unity has particularly come under the spotlight—and at times we are as likely to find ourselves at the heart of other people's projections of disunity, and pulled in different and incompatible directions by those we desire to serve. Frank knows that more than most.

Yet I have been impressed by the gracious way he has handled these competing, often mutually exclusive, demands. Leaders are also servants of the church. While exercising leadership, Frank has also allowed himself to be led by the decisions taken within ECUSA—which has one of the most open, transparent, and democratic systems of any Province in the Communion. He has been faithful in defending ECUSA to others. (And here we should not underestimate the seriousness with which he holds that the Spirit can indeed speak to the church when it sincerely meets in council, and that it is not only leaders whom the Lord gifts with insight and understanding.) Yet he had again and again also gone the extra mile in trying to convey the breadth and depth of debates over the years, and the particular demands that the North American churches face in discerning what the gospel of reconciliation means in their own societies. In the years I have known him, Frank has always tried to make space for all sides to express their views, and for all sides to have opportunities to come to understand better the views of others. At the Primates' meetings, he has walked that difficult tightrope between openness, honesty, and flexibility in our discussions, while remaining true to the decisions of his church.

Living in this painful tension is too often the lot of leadership, much as we would desire a unity where all are in agreement over what constitutes the truth. Yet in Jesus Christ we find consolation. For though, as Paul tells us, all things hold together in him, he is also the one who said that he came not to bring peace but a sword.

For it is not up to us to effect reconciliation—that is Jesus' task, and his delight. It is God's work, though we share in this ministry. And no matter how important we may become within the institutional church, it still remains God's work and not ours. It is for us to be faithful and obedient in expressing the gospel message entrusted to us. There are so many occasions when I have remembered that with relief!

There is more to remember. God in Christ is indeed reconciling the world to himself, and he does so not counting our sins, our shortcomings, our weaknesses, our failings, against us.[8]

To express the vast riches of what this means requires us to believe and trust it ourselves in all its fullness. We must grasp that it is true for us—and know ourselves reconciled, know that our sins are not counted against us, and stop counting them for ourselves! And we must know that God is not counting against them the sins of those whom he is reconciling to himself—so therefore neither must we count these. We ask the Lord to write these truths in our hearts so we may pursue a more Christ-like waging of reconciliation.

This is not to say that we consider ourselves or others to be sinless, for that would indeed be to deceive ourselves and them. Rather, it is to live in the glorious liberty of the gospel that has broken the power of sin, and the death it brings—to know that in Christ sin can be transcended and we can all experience his resurrection life within us, redeeming us from what we were and transforming us to what we were called to be.

Such knowledge is more than can be achieved through intellectual reflection or human willpower! It comes only through attentiveness to the living experience of the Lord's reconciling love in our lives. We must let our God love us. We must learn to receive and accept and explore the truth of our "belovedness,"[9] to use one of Frank's words. The love of God unfreezes our hearts, eases the pains of our own inadequacies, and frees us to reach out as channels of that same love to others.

Often we speak of the "prophetic voice of the church in the world"—that has probably been the correct term to use both in the church's opposition to apartheid and in the rebuilding that is following in South Africa, a place where some degree of awareness of the spiritual dimension remains integral to the life of the majority. Yet when I read Frank's words, when I hear him speak, it seems to me that his is the "*mystic* voice of the church in the world." I believe this is the voice that is often hardest to hear, and yet which most needs to be heard, in the secularization of so much of Western society.

Mysticism, said Elie Wiesel, "means the way to attain knowledge. It's close to philosophy, except in philosophy you go horizontally whereas in mysticism you go vertically."[10]

Frank certainly goes vertically. Yet he combines this with the horizontal—as we have heard in his articulate criticisms of American policy, both at home and abroad. His message is clear—as he made plain at his fifth anniversary as Presiding Bishop. Every Christian is called at baptism to "the work of repair, rebuilding and renewing" the world. This work calls for "adopting God's point of view" instead of the limited perspective of self or nation. "If we are truly a nation 'under God,' as we say we are, then God's perspective rather than our own self-interest will animate both our national life and our being in the world. Otherwise we had better abandon that claim altogether and admit that our power is the source of our own divinity."[11]

The American critic Gail Sheehy has said, "The secrets of a leader lie in the tests he has faced over the whole course of his life, and the habits of action he develops in meeting those tests." Frank's life as Presiding Bishop has brought many tests. And in those we have seen how his preaching and teaching, his passion for God's justice and God's reconciliation, are an eloquent witness to the habits he has developed, in following in the footsteps of his Lord.

Notes

1. Rev. 15:3.
2. Micah 6:8.
3. 2 Cor. 5:18.

4. Sermon preached at the Consecration of Pierre Whalon in Rome on 1 November 2001.

5. On Waging Reconciliation, Statement by the House of Bishops, 26 September 2001.

6. Sermon preached at the Cathedral Church of St. John the Divine, New York City on 6 March 2005.

7. R. S. Thomas, in his poem "Roger Bacon."

8. 2 Cor. 5:19.

9. Sermon preached in Austin, Texas, on 13 February 2005.

10. From an interview with Elie Wiesel in *Writers at Work: The Paris Review Interviews,* eighth series, ed. George Plimpton (New York: Penguin Books, 1988).

11. Sermon preached at Washington National Cathedral on 12 January 2003.

Called to Reconciliation:
The Challenge of Globalization
and the Anglican Communion

Ian T. Douglas

NINE DAYS AFTER the terrorist attacks on New York and Washington, the House of Bishops of the Episcopal Church issued a pastoral statement from their fall 2001 House of Bishops Meeting in Burlington, Vermont. The statement was entitled "On Waging Reconciliation" and said in part:

> We are called to self-examination and repentance: the willingness to change direction, to open our hearts and give room to God's compassion as it seeks to bind up, to heal, and to make all things new and whole. God's project, in which we participate by virtue of our baptism, is the ongoing work of reordering and transforming the patterns of our common life so they may reveal God's justness—not as an abstraction but in bread for the hungry and clothing for the naked. . . . Let us therefore wage reconciliation. Let us offer our gifts for the carrying out of God's ongoing work of reconciliation, healing

and making all things new. To this we pledge
ourselves and call our church.[1]

The bishops' pledge and call to "wage reconciliation"
(which was drafted primarily by Presiding Bishop Frank
Griswold) was a radical response to the atrocities of 9/11.
While many in the United States immediately sought
to punish the perpetrators of the evil of 9/11, with some
leaders even calling for a new crusade against terrorism,
the bishops instead looked at themselves first and declared that they and all in the world are in need of forgiveness.[2] At a time when the rest of the United States
was calling for retribution and revenge, the bishops set
out on a path of amendment of life and reconciliation.
What led the bishops to such a countercultural position? What did the bishops' words hold for a world that
is both drawn together and torn apart by the forces of
globalization?

Christian Leadership in a World of Globalization

Every June during his years as Presiding Bishop Frank
Griswold has invited a group of eight to ten theologians
to meet with him for four days of informal conversations on a designated topic. The purpose of these gatherings has been for his own learning: to resource him
to ask new questions and to see new possibilities. The
focus of the conversations in 2001 was global mission.
During the 1998 Lambeth Conference of Bishops, just
months after he became Presiding Bishop, he had seen
the possibilities and problems of globalization played
out in that meeting, and since then he had been ponder-
ing the implications for the Anglican Communion. The

conversation with the theologians and missiologists he gathered in June 2001 focused on the challenges of globalization from the perspective of the mission, or more specifically the *missio Dei,* God's mission.

Having found the conversation extremely fruitful, he asked several of those who had been with him in June to deliver papers at the September 2001 meeting of the House of Bishops and the Bishops' Spouses. Long before the terrorist attacks the topic for the meeting had been determined: God's Mission in a Time of Globalization. Therefore, it is not by chance that out of that meeting came a vision of reconciliation in a world of globalization. It could be said that a major impetus for Bishop Griswold's central commitment to the *missio Dei,* understood as the reconciliation and restoration of all people to unity with God and each other in Christ (drawing on the Catechism in the Book of Common Prayer), was these 2001 gatherings.

In the midst of ecclesiastical struggles over human sexuality Bishop Griswold has continued to hold up the vision and possibility that the divisions in the Church, along with the alienation and hurt in the world, have already been reconciled and restored through the life, death, and resurrection of Jesus Christ. For him the *missio Dei,* the mission of God, in which all Christians participate through our baptism and the power of the Holy Spirit, is to make all things new through the love of God in Christ. What then is the specific call of the Episcopal Church and the Anglican Communion, given the challenges of globalization? What charism (to use a favorite term of Bishop Griswold's) does Anglicanism embody that might prove life-giving for a world torn apart by poverty, war, disease, and religious conflict?

The Challenge of Globalization

Globalization is a term that raises many different images and ideas depending on the context in which the word is used. For many, globalization often means the world-wide spread of a neo-liberal economic system under-girded by unbridled access to a single global economic market. In such an understanding of globalization, the rich seem to profit at the expense of the poor, and the gulf between those who have and those who have not continues to grow with no seeming end in sight. Many see such economic globalization, the global reach of the free-market system with no checks and balances, as an evil that is fundamentally corrupt and unsustainable.

But globalization need not be framed in such terms. Globalization can also be considered morally neutral. Thus seen, globalization is simply the process by which anything, any movement, any phenomenon, becomes global. The Harvard economist Richard Parker has argued articulately that globalization as a phenomenon "is at least half a million years old, and began when our pre-historic ancestors walked out of Africa, into the Middle East, Europe, and Asia—and eventually Australia and the Americas."[3]

Parker believes that the process of the worldwide growth and spread of humanity is inevitable, and not necessarily a negative phenomenon. He does argue, however, that over the last 500 years, what he describes as the era of "Europeanization," there have been incred-ible abuses of the peoples and lands in what were con-sidered the colonies of European and North American nation states.[4] The project of European and North American colonization that subjugated the peoples of

Africa, Asia, Latin America, and the Pacific led to a superimposition of Western economic, cultural, political, and religious norms. Unfortunately then, the same forces from the West that had been silencing the voices and undermining any push to self-determination of the global South continued unchecked in the "postcolonial" era of unbridled free-market economics.

"Europeanization" and Western colonial reach have been immensely furthered by advances in global communication and its supporting technologies over the last century and a half. While timely worldwide communication began to emerge with the advent of the rotary printing press and Samuel Morse's invention of the telegraph in the nineteenth century, the explosion of rapid digital communication over the World Wide Web during the last few decades has radically speeded the process of globalization.[5] Today no corner of the world is beyond the reach of digital communication. The use of information technology has spread, linking economic markets such that billions and billions of dollars can flow immediately between time zones. The global market never sleeps. The loss of the bipolar world of Cold War days, along with the demise of socialism as a viable economic and social alternative, has led to the emergence of an unconstrained capitalist free-market global economic system.

A result of the global digital information flow and the single market economy is a worldwide cultural hegemony that asserts a singular norm of flavor, taste, and desire around the world, thereby discounting the plurality of local cultural expressions. The sociologist George Ritzer has described this homogenization process as the "McDonaldization" of society.[6] In the McDonaldized world, all people eat the same hamburgers and drink the same milkshakes no matter where they live. The same Starbucks coffee or Gap jeans can be found in Baltimore, Buenos Aires, Berlin, Brussels, Beijing, or Bombay.

In the McDonaldized world, those at the margins and without power suffer most. It is they who must struggle to reassert their own ways of understanding the world and fight for their own means of production and sustenance. In the McDonalized world the local, the particular, and the homegrown are always vulnerable to the interests and power of the global.

Today we are seeing the local push back against the forces of globalization. The reassertion of the local can be clearly seen when indigenous peoples assert their treaty rights to ancestral lands, and when, for example, India refuses to let Coca-Cola into their country in order to protect their national soft drink industry. In clear and also subtle ways this push-back of the local against the global is at work when individuals refuse to give up their identity and their ability to make their own choices in order to protect what is most precious and of value in their own context and cultural ways of making meaning.

The push-back of the local can either be a healthy form of resistance to globalization or, at the worst, can lead to a new tyranny of the local, in which all possibilities and opportunities for new growth and access in the global world are sacrificed on the altar of the single identity politics of the local.[7] The negative forces of the local against the global are not limited to young anarchists throwing rocks through storefronts at meetings of the World Trade Organization. One might see the atrocities of 9/11 as a response of the local against the global. Were not the targets of the terrorists what they considered the symbols of globalization, namely the economic, military, and political institutions of the World Trade Center, the Pentagon, and the United States government? Just as the forces of globalization can be either life-affirming or destructive depending on the circumstances and the context, so too the push-back from the local can be healthy *or* destructive.

In the globalized world we thus see the twin competing phenomenon of the worldwide reach of mono-economic, mono-cultural realities and the attendant push-back of local, particular, peoples and their cultures.[8] The question facing our global village is this: How can a single economic and cultural system, driven by the worldwide capitalist market and facilitated by digital communication, function in such a way that the voices and cultural realities of any one people or context are not lost? In other words: How can the global live with the local, and the local live with the global, without either one or the other seeking to dominate with a destructive and life-denying result? How can the global and the local coexist, and even thrive together, such that each can better inform and add to the life-affirming possibilities of the other?

The Anglican Communion and the Call to God's Mission

The challenge before the Anglican Communion today is very similar to, and not unrelated to, the challenge of globalization.[9] While some might see human sexuality as the key issue before the Anglican Communion, the deeper issue before Anglicans around the world is how a family of 38 national or regional churches in 164 countries with over 75 million members can learn to live together as one global communion given all of our different localities and expressions of the gospel. In other words, how can the particular unfolding of the Holy Spirit in any one local Anglican church coexist with the global witness of the church catholic as expressed in the wider Anglican Communion? Or conversely: How can the global witness of the church catholic as expressed in the wider Anglican Communion coexist with the particular unfolding of the Holy Spirit in any one local Anglican church?

Recent divisions in the Anglican Communion with respect to issues in human sexuality have exacerbated the tensions between the local and the global in the Anglican Communion and cast a bright light onto the negative aspects of globalization. More specifically the consent to the election of the Bishop of New Hampshire, a homosexual man living in a committed relationship with another man, at the General Convention of the Episcopal Church in 2003, and the authorization of the development of rites for the blessing of same-sex unions in the Diocese of New Westminster in the Anglican Church of Canada, show how local responses to gospel imperatives and the leading of the Holy Spirit in some localities (New Hampshire and New Westminster) have geopolitical ramifications for the Anglican Communion at the global level. While the dioceses of New Hampshire and New Westminster were trying to respond faithfully to key leadership and pastoral concerns within their own context, their decisions had ramifications for the wider global church. These ramifications become even more pronounced when those opposed to the full inclusion of gay and lesbian people in the Church in North America, aided by instant digital global communication and international airline routes, joined forces with those in other parts of the world who shared their views. What has resulted is the classic globalization struggle over identity and authority. In the globalized world the central questions are: Who is in charge? Who has the power? Is it the local or is it the global? Who gets to say who is a faithful Anglican and what is good and right in the Anglican Communion? Can local initiatives and responses to contextual leadings of the Holy Spirit—whether they be the embrace of gay and lesbian persons in North America or all-night vigils including ecstatic Spirit possession and walking on fire as liturgical expressions in central Africa—coexist and maybe even complement the global catholic witness of the Anglican Communion?[10]

Some in the inner-ecclesial fights over the place of gay and lesbian people in the Church want to make the battles in the Anglican Communion about the single identity politics of human sexuality. Others, while acknowledging these disagreements as presenting causes, see the deeper issue as being about the nature of the church. This latter perspective is represented in the Windsor Report, produced by the Lambeth Commission on Communion. The Lambeth Commission was called into being by the primates of the Anglican Communion (senior bishops of each of the 38 churches in the Anglican Communion) at the meeting called by the Archbishop of Canterbury in October 2003 in response to the Episcopal Church's consent to the election in the Diocese of New Hampshire. The Commission, however, was not charged with solving questions about human sexuality but rather with considering "ways in which communion and understanding could be enhanced where serious differences threatened the life of a diverse worldwide church. In short, they looked at how the Anglican Communion could address relationships between its component parts in a true spirit of communion."[11] The Lambeth Commission's brief thus reflected the quintessential challenge presented by globalization, that is, negotiating the competing realities of local particularities while maintaining a wholeness to the witness of the church catholic.

The Windsor Report of the Lambeth Commission on Communion is a significant and complex study of Anglican ecclesiology. It outlines both the possibilities and difficulties of working through differences in a global family of churches. Written by an international body of seventeen theologians, lawyers, priests, bishops, and archbishops from fourteen different Anglican churches around the world, the Report itself embraces a variety of voices and perspectives. A close analysis of the many findings and recommendations of the Windsor Report is beyond the scope of this essay.[12] In general, however, the Windsor Report advances a more structural or instrumentalist approach to dealing with the globalization challenge of the local and global. Tightening up the "four instruments of unity" (namely the office of the Archbishop of Canterbury, the Lambeth Conference of Bishops, the Anglican Consultative Council, and the Primates Meeting), and investing in them greater power to determine the "limits of Anglican diversity," is a major thrust of the Windsor Report.[13] The question, however, must be asked: Is the local/global challenge best served through a structural or instrumentalist approach? Do the "structural adjustment polices" of the Windsor Report adequately serve a truly global family of churches embracing a vast plurality of cultures, peoples and particularities?

Tightening up the instruments of unity (now understood as the "instruments of Communion" beginning with the 2005 meeting of the Anglican Consultative Council) gives one or another of the "instruments" more power to adjudicate complex differences from a top down position. Any attempt to enforce a global norm on the work of the Holy Spirit in any one locality, however, runs the risk of advancing a hegemonic, mono-cultural view of the Anglican Communion. On the other hand the super-assertion of the experience and decisions of any one local church, without regard for the reality of the church catholic, runs the risk of fomenting separation and schism. So what is an Anglican or the Anglican Communion to do? What then are the healthy models of communion in Anglicanism where local particularities and global realties interact in a mutually beneficial and life-affirming manner?

There are at least four recent examples of Anglicans meeting the challenge of globalization by coming together in relationships across difference to serve God's mission of reconciliation.[14] In each of these four cases, the local experience of Christians in one place contributed to a fuller expression of the Gospel in the church catholic while not sacrificing the integrity and specificity of the motions of the Holy Spirit in the local context.

The first example is the united witness of the Anglican Communion in support of the efforts of South African Anglicans and others in combating apartheid.

Archbishop Emeritus of Cape Town Desmond Tutu is often quoted as saying that without seventy million Anglicans around the world standing behind him and watching over him, he could never have been as bold as he was in confronting the evils of apartheid in his local context.

A second example of Anglicans coming together in relationships across difference to serve God's mission is the way the churches of the Anglican Communion, following the invitation of the 1988 Lambeth Conference of Bishops, each lived into the dream of a Decade of Evangelism. While there was no one uniform set program of evangelism for the whole Anglican Communion, each Anglican church pursued various evangelistic forms of outreach uniquely tailored to its own local context. As a result, from 1988 through 1998 the saving good news of Jesus Christ was heard in many more cultures and languages than at any other time in the history of Anglicanism.[15]

A third example is the way Anglicans rallied behind the Jubilee 2000 campaign to alleviate international debt to the highest-indebted poor countries of the world. Following the Lambeth Conference of 1998 Anglican bishops and other church leaders from across the Anglican Communion cooperated with ecumenical and government leaders in moving the United States Congress and President Bill Clinton to enact a debt-relief package that immediately cancelled one billion dollars (U.S.) in bilateral debts. This same bill became the framework for an international agreement by the then Group of Seven—the largest industrialized countries in the world—resulting in the leveraging of an estimated additional twenty-seven billion dollars in debt relief.

The fourth example is the way that the churches of the Anglican Communion, beginning with the Primates Meeting of 2001 in Kanuga, North Carolina and then bolstered by All Africa Anglican AIDS Planning Framework, have begun to come together in relationships across our differences to overcome the scourge of the HIV/AIDS pandemic in our many localities and contexts.[16] Recently this call to fight the HIV/AIDS pandemic has been attached to a larger vision for the fullness of God's realm as represented in the Millennium Development Goals (MDG's) embraced by all of the countries of the United Nations. The Archbishop of Canterbury and the Archbishop of Cape Town, Njongonkulu Ndungane, have been particularly articulate in calling Anglicans to come together in relationships across our differences to serve God's mission of reconciliation as expressed in the MDG's.[17]

Whether it be combating apartheid in South Africa, proclaiming the Gospel of Jesus in new cultural realities through the Decade of Evangelism, lobbying for international debt relief, or working to meet the MDG's, the Anglican Communion represents one of the most liberating responses to the challenge of globalization in the world today. The Anglican Communion is truly gifted with a universal global commonality in Christ that affirms the particularities of the Incarnation and the work of the Holy Spirit in each of our local contexts.

The fact that Anglicans demonstrably can come together in relationships across difference to serve God's mission of reconciliation indeed offers hope for our divided world. And, this is a most necessary hope: if the Anglican Communion cannot meet the challenge of globalization, given our commonality in Christ and the empowerment of the Holy Spirit, then how can any other body or institution be expected to do so? If we Anglicans cannot continue to live together with all of our differences and all of our possibilities, then what sign will we give to a world that is struggling to negotiate the local/global dynamics of globalization? Thus, we might say that the Anglican Communion is the canary in the mineshaft of globalization.

Perhaps the bishops of the Episcopal Church did have it right in their September 2001 call to self-examination and repentance. Their words offer hope and direction for the Episcopal Church and the Anglican Communion to meet the challenge of globalization: "Let us therefore wage reconciliation. Let us offer our gifts for the carrying out of God's ongoing work of reconciliation, healing and making all things new. To this we pledge ourselves and call our church."

Notes

1. "On Waging Reconciliation," in Ian T. Douglas, ed. *Waging Reconciliation: God's Mission in a Time of Globalization and Crisis* (New York: Church Publishing, Inc., 2002), xi.

2. This call for reconciliation was criticized by some who thought it was naïve and not well reasoned. *U.S. News & World Report* commentator John Leo was particularly upset with the bishops' call to wage reconciliation. His commentary "Turning a blind eye to evil," in the October 12, 2001 issue of *U.S. News,* accused the House of Bishops of producing "an unusually disgraceful statement on the terrorist attacks."

3. Richard Parker, "Globalization, The Social Gospel and Christian leadership Today," in Douglas, ed., *Waging Reconciliation,* 79.

4. Ibid., 82.

5. Ibid., 81.

6. George Ritzer, *The McDonaldization of Society: An Inves-*

tigation Into the Changing Character of Contemporary Social Life (Thousand Oaks, California: Pine Forge Press, 1993).

7. The classic study of this tension between the local and the global is Benjamin Barber, *Jihad vs McWorld* (New York: Ballantine, 2001.)

8. Christopher Duraisingh describes these twin phenomena as the centripetal and centrifugal forces of globalization. See Christopher Duraisingh, "Encountering Difference in a Plural World: A Pentecost Paradigm for Mission," in Douglas, ed., *Waging Reconciliation,* 174–175.

9. For the role of how religion (specifically Judaism) can play a constructive role in negotiating the tensions between the local and the global, see Jonathan Sacks, *The Dignity of Difference: How to Avoid the Clash of Civilizations* (London and New York: Continuum, 2002.)

10. For a substantial investigation into these African liturgical practices see Titus Presler, *Transfigured Night: Mission and Culture in Zimbabwe's Vigil Movement* (Pretoria, Univ. of South Africa Press, 1999).

11. The Lambeth Commission on Communion, *The Windsor Report* (London, The Anglican Communion Office, 2004) 5.

12. For a fuller discussion of my views on the Windsor Report see Ian T. Douglas and Paul Zahl, *Understanding the Windsor Report: Two Leaders in the American Church Speak Across the Divide* (New York: Church Publishing, 2005); and Ian T. Douglas, "An American Reflects on the Windsor Report" *Journal of Anglican Studies* 3.2 (December, 2005): 155–179.

13. Ascribing more power to one or another of the "four instruments" in order to determine the "limits of Anglican diversity" is not a new idea with the Lambeth Commission on Communion. The specific bolstering of the instruments was taken up at the 1998 Lambeth Conference in Resolution III.6: on "Instruments of The Anglican Communion." Resolution III.6 advanced the role of primates, seeking to make them the episcopal members of the Anglican Consultative Council and also asking "the Primates Meeting, under the Presidency of the Archbishop of Canterbury, (to) include among its responsibilities . . . intervention in cases of exceptional emergency which are incapable of internal resolution within provinces and giving of guidelines on the limits of Anglican diversity. . ." *The Official Report of the Lambeth Conference of 1998* (Harrisburg, Pennsylvania:

Morehouse Publishing for the Anglican Communion, 1999), 396–397.

14. Missiological underpinnings for an emerging Anglican ecclesiology in light of the challenges of globalization are discussed in detail in Ian T. Douglas, "Anglicans Gathering for God's Mission: A Missiological Ecclesiology for the Anglican Communion," *Journal of Anglican Studies* 2.2 (December 2004): 9–40; and Ian T. Douglas, "Authority, Unity and Mission in the Windsor Report" *Anglican Theological Review* 87 #4 (Fall, 2005): 567–574.

15. The contributions of the Decade of Evangelism are celebrated by MISSIO, the Inter-Anglican Standing Commission on Mission and Evangelism in their final report: Eleanor Johnson and John Clark, eds., *Anglicans in Mission: A Transforming Journey* (London: SPCK, 2000).

16. "Our Vision, Our Hope: The First Step: All Africa Anglican AIDS Planning Framework," Anglican Communion News Service #2601, 22 August, 2001, http://anglicancommunion.org/acns/acnsarchive/acns2600/acns2601.html.

17. The best articulation of the missiological rationale for the MDG's as expressed by key Anglican voices is found in: Sabina Alkire and Edmund Newell, *What Can One Person Do? Faith to Heal a Broken World* (New York: Church Publishing, Inc., 2005).

Making Way for the Image of God: A Spirituality of Reconciliation

Denise M. Ackermann

Introduction

As a white South African woman, a theologian, and an Anglican, I have been challenged by the complex and daunting task of reconciling across race, gender, and class differences for as long as I can remember. Looking back over the forty years of apartheid and the last eleven years of democratic rule, I see failures, threads of hope, and above all the abiding certainty that in my life, reconciliation across anger and difference is a gift from God and not something of my own making. This gift, undeserved and gratefully accepted, lies at the core of what I understand by spirituality.

My erstwhile spiritual director Francis Cull recalled an old rabbi who said, "An angel walks before every human being saying: 'Make way, make way for the image of God.'" This contribution in honor of Bishop Frank Griswold attempts to heed the angel's cry by describing aspects of an embodied spirituality of reconciliation. Reconciliation has many faces—a fact I shall refer to below—but I shall focus on reconciliation among Christians, a dire need in our fractious church and one that has confronted the ministry of Frank Griswold. His life and service to his church have been grounded in his spirituality and I want, therefore, from my distant place, to share these reflections on a spirituality of reconciliation.

Understanding Reconciliation

In Christianity there is no one clear view of reconciliation. Context and circumstance dictate our understanding of it. However, reconciliation is central to being a Christian trying to live in relationship with others and with God. Flora Keshgegian in her work *Redeeming Memories* argues that through the power of Jesus Christ we not only encounter God but we become participants in the divine through the mediation of the Holy Spirit. Such participation is embodied.

> Our redemption is a concrete process that brings us fully into a different kind of relationship. Such relationship has been described as reconciliation and right relation. Reconciliation implies right relation—that which has been out of harmony or off balance or at odds is brought back into right relationship.[1]

Reconciliation thus takes place within the framework of the redemptive narrative of our relationship with the God of grace and mercy and is expressed in the embodiment of right relations—with God, ourselves, others, and our world. Reconciliation is the work of

God, who restores our brokenness so that we may live with justice and love in community. Keshgegian's stress on the relational aspect of reconciliation is particularly valid where prejudice, estrangement, and dogmatically held views have alienated people in the church from one another.

For me reconciliation means a tangible action, a contextual practice involving our whole being, something we choose to become involved in and celebrate before we explain it. It is not, in the first instance, a theological doctrine, but a process that we engage in as God's hands in the world.

Reconciliation as Change

Reconciliation requires change. Not surprisingly, the question then arises: Can human beings really change? Can we fractious members of the body of Christ change and become truly one? Dorothee Sölle's reply to this question is scathing: "I see this question as true atheism. Whoever poses such a question, whoever believes that human beings cannot change, does not believe in God. In the Bible what we call 'change' is really 'redemption'" [my translation].[2] Overcoming discord and reconciling across our differences is, therefore, possible if one accepts that human beings can change.

What resources do we have to propel us towards change? Our most accessible and treasured resource is the gospel. The gospel provides motivation by setting before us a story of what has happened and what will happen. Confronted with the past and the future, our attention is drawn to the ethical quality of our present actions and we are invited to meaningful participation in changing the world. God's reconciliation in Jesus Christ is our model and sets the pattern for us to emulate by pointing to the centrality of reconciliation. God crosses the bridge to us, not by demanding, but by reaching out in grace.

Embodied Change

Why *embodied* change? We live embodied lives. The fact that we can see, hear, think, touch, smell, and feel is the source of what we know. All reality and all knowledge are mediated through our bodies. All theological reflection starts with the body. It is nonsensical to think that theology or spirituality are separate from the concreteness of the human body and concerned solely with some abstract realm of the spirit. Reconciliation itself is not abstract. It needs to be absorbed in minds, articulated on tongues, visibly demonstrated in bodily acts, and embraced in hearts.

God offers us reconciliation in the Incarnation. "The Word became flesh and lived among us" is a statement of faith that God became "embodied" as one of us. Incarnation is about meeting God in the body. Yet Christians still struggle with the very bodiliness of our salvation. Centuries of theological thinking have belittled the body and relegated it to a lower status than the spirit. This I fail to understand. The Christian idea of reconciliation (and salvation) has no meaning outside the body and its well-being. When we speak of the Word who became flesh, we are not only hungering for healing and wholeness, but we are claiming the totality of reconciliation promised to us in and through the

Word. Our bodily experience is the fundamental realm of the experience of God.

An Embodied Spirituality of Reconciliation

The church is called to be an agent for change and bearer of the Christian message of reconciliation. Sadly the church itself has often been stricken with strife that imperils its true nature as the one body of Christ and damages our witness to a world in need of reconciliation. Christians have no option but to be reconcilers. Such is our calling. It requires a spirituality that is tuned to God's intention for the church and its witness in the world. So where to start?

First we start with an incontrovertible truth: *God is the author of reconciliation.* Reconciliation is a gift from God; it is not earned. It is accepted, not deserved. The acceptance of this truth means waking up to God's loving intention for our daily lives. We are to be reconciled to God, to our true selves, to one another, and to all of creation. God gives, we receive; and in the receiving, awareness of God's mercy and love enables us to begin the process of being reconciled to ourselves and to one another. We change, moving away from self-centeredness, prejudice, and estrangement to the truth of our identity that has been hidden in the love of God. We may choose not to be the real persons God intends us to be. Or we may choose to work together with God in the creation of our true identity and destiny to be a reconciled people. Reconciliation in the church requires people who, in discovering themselves, discover God in themselves, enabling them to be reconciled to themselves and to others.

Second, our awareness of God's reconciling intention brings us to the thorniest part of reconciliation, which is forgiveness. It is hard to forgive, and often harder to accept forgiveness. Hasty forgiveness can seem like a betrayal of the past, an effort to wipe out painful memories in order to achieve cheap reconciliation without honoring such memories—a kind of tawdry "forgive and forget." Then as Keshgegian remarks, forgiveness "gets in the way of remembering fully."[3] There is no "forgive and forget." "Remember and forgive" is more appropriate.[4] This requires forbearance from revenge. Only then may memories be redeemed to the extent that reconciliation becomes a possibility.

It is necessary to distinguish between divine and human forgiveness. God forgives sins, not simply because God has the power to do so, but because God is infinite love. We are not required to change in order to be forgiven by God. We cannot earn God's forgiveness. Instead we can become whole because we are forgiven. Confession is not some vain attempt to make us acceptable to God, but an acceptance that enables us to renarrate our lives so that we are capable of appropriating God's forgiveness into our lives as forgiven and forgiving people.[5] We can then live the grace of reconciliation granted us through the work of the Holy Spirit, who judges, consoles, and guides us into new ways.

God's forgiveness comes first. Human forgiveness starts from a different point, namely, through acknowledging the truth of our unreconciled lives. Being able to forgive is in Robert Schreiter's words "an act of freedom."[6] It involves choice. But first a word of caution. Some acts are so evil and destructive that forgiveness seems impossible. Premature speech about forgiveness and reconciliation can fail to acknowledge the moral force of righteous anger. When we decide to forgive we decide to become free from the power of the past. We do not forgive because those who have wronged us have repented. We acknowledge our wounding and decide to move on. We choose a different future.

Forgiveness does not mean that we wipe out the past or excuse a wrongdoer. Rather it asserts that the balance of power has passed from the wrong that was committed, from the violator to the victim. It is the victim's sole prerogative to decide to forgive. Forgiveness is an active, willed change of heart that succeeds in overcoming naturally felt feelings of anger, resentment, vengeance, and hatred. It has a gift-like quality. The decision to forgive is the point at which divine and human forgiveness intersect. If God had not forgiven us first, human forgiveness would not be possible.

Third, moving through this process of awareness, acknowledgment, and forgiveness then brings us to the inescapable need for *justice.* Reconciliation is about restoring justice. There is no consistent understanding of justice in the modern world. We usually understand justice in a way that suits our individual and collective interests. In South Africa today justice bears many labels: punitive, corrective, distributive, retributive, remedial, restorative, practical, and redemptive are but some. I choose to understand justice as restoring "right relationship." Restorative rather than punitive justice is that which remakes what God intends for us—that our human worth be affirmed and upheld in right mutual relationship with one another. Restorative justice rebuilds communities of right relationship, and its goal is healing and reconciliation. What would it mean for the church to bear witness to restorative justice? It would certainly mean the re-ordering of power relations in church structures. A good place to start would be to get our house in order in terms of just gender relations!

Fourth, we believe that we are all made in *the image of God*. That is to say that love is the reason for my existence because God is love. In Thomas Merton's words: "Love is my true identity. Selflessness is my true self. Love is my true character. Love is my name."[7] Therefore anything that I do or think or say that is not purely for the love of God, says Merton, cannot lead to peace, reconciliation, or fulfillment.

To embody the image of God is to be holy as God is holy. The very thought of being holy can at first glance seem absurd. Can we possibly be holy? Feelings of unworthiness surface. Why? Are we instinctively recoiling from a demand that we feel we cannot meet? Or are we at heart obstructing the working of God's Spirit in each of us? Whatever the answers to these questions are, the idea of holiness is central to our faith. Our scriptures do not allow us to avoid the call to holiness. In fact, holiness cannot be acquired. We already possess holiness. We must live in our holiness.

In the New Testament, Jesus is the revelation of the holy—in a manger, a carpenter's son, crucified as a criminal. He was born and died on days that were not then holy but on days that were made holy by the way he lived them. From the raw material of everyday life, Jesus fashioned his holiness. So the apostle John calls Jesus Christ the "Holy One of God" (John 6:69). The Holy One of God is the One who abides in us. Abiding in Christ who is holy can mean nothing other than that we too are called to holiness. Thus believers are "saints," "a holy priesthood," "partakers of the divine nature." For Christians "the holy" is never just the church, the chapel, the shrine, or the place set apart where only a few may enter. It is never simply a holy day, or a holy woman or man. Holiness is at the core of every Christian's identity, both personally and as members of the holy priesthood of believers. Holiness is not an optional extra; rather it is the whole point of creation that enables us to pray "Our Father, Hallowed be your name."

It is both encouraging and comforting, although at the same time unnerving, to know that our call to holiness comes from the Holy One who longs for us to be holy as God is holy. It is a simple matter that is no less than everything. It calls for a renewing of our minds. We must begin to think about our visions and our vocations in terms of holiness, for such thinking is, in fact, thinking about God. The journey to holiness is the discovery of what it means to be made in the image of God. God is love. Love is my true identity. God is holy. Holiness is my true being. To live in my holiness is to live in God, hearing the angel's cry: "Make way, make way for the image of God."

Fifth, an embodied spirituality of reconciliation is nurtured by the discipline of silence and solitude. The discipline of silence is cultivated in every religious tradition that I know. For instance, the Hebrew word for the presence of God—*shekinah*—has the same root as the Arabic word for that pause or silence that a pious Muslim observes in the course of daily prayers. The longing for stillness is not a longing for pleasure, happiness, or peace. It is a desire for encounter, for moving away from words *to* and words *about* God, to waiting *upon* God.

Times of stillness, silence, and solitude are vital for nurturing a spirituality of reconciliation. Words come readily to our lips, often too readily. We shy away from trusting God in silence and quietness. It is just much easier to keep the chatter going. Ambrose knew this when he instructed Augustine: "I have seen many," he said, "who were saved by silence but none who were saved by chatter." We are too often preoccupied instead of quiet; restless instead of still; noisy instead of silent; overburdened and hurtling along unable to stop—all rendering us incapable of hearing the call of the Holy One. Thomas Merton said, "My life is listening. God's is speaking."[8] In the struggle to be still with God, our utter poverty is revealed to us. All our plans, visions, talk, and spiritual ambitions are useless, for all that matters is God's glory. Glimpsing our poverty is a blessing that shatters us. Then, for the first time, we see the magnitude of God's mercy and our hearts swell with gratitude.

But soon, very soon, holiness demands to be put to work in the service of love. Mere withdrawal and quiet without returning to the active work of reconciliation will only lead to spiritual inertia or even worse, to a pride that finds pleasure in contemplating our "holiness." The spiritual life is a constant movement between times of silence and solitude, and times of active participation as God's hands in this world.

Sixth, the truth of our holiness raises a difficult question: "Am I prepared for sacrifice?" There is an old saying about any task you undertake, that when you have done 95 percent of the work you are only halfway there. This is true in our quest for reconciliation. The further we go, the more intense the demands upon us become. Paul speaks of our lives as "a living sacrifice" (Rom. 12:1). We recoil immediately, for we know that sacrifice entails suffering. We know, through the person of Jesus Christ, that the climax of the whole creation is self-sacrifice. The truth is that we are very much beginners; we are neither spontaneous nor pure, and we shrink from suffering. But if we long for reconciliation, we can begin with small, often unnoticed, sacrificial acts, and be courageous enough to embrace their consequences.

Finally, a church that seeks to embody reconciliation has a valuable asset in the power of ritual. Ritual can express deeply felt but seldom-articulated feelings, because its drama can speak of that for which we have no words. Rituals can hold the promise of healing broken relationships. The Eucharist is extraordinarily significant for reconciliation. In the Eucharist the themes touched on thus far come together: the promise of change, the embodied reality of our faith, the need for forgiveness and restorative justice, and the restoration of relationship given to us as common bearers of the image of God. We not only share in the "one bread" of the communion, but we commit ourselves to share ourselves with those who are needy, alienated, or simply "other," because this is what it means to become "bread for the world." This is by implication the impetus for restoring community.

The Eucharist is the bodily practice of grace. Suffering and alienated bodies can partake of the feast. Bodies are absolutely central to the Eucharist, our bodies and the body of Christ. Participating in this rite unites our bodies in a mysteriously wonderful way. "The bread that we break, is it not a sharing in the body of Christ? Because there is one bread, we who are many are one body, for we all partake of the one bread" (1 Cor. 10:16, 17). Our differences melt away as we are all drawn into the one body of the risen Christ.

After participating in the Eucharist, we join in thanks and then commit ourselves as "living sacrifices in Jesus Christ" to live and work in the world to God's praise and glory—a noble, moving undertaking. The significance of both the gift given in Christ in the Eucharist and the fulfillment of that gift in the future lies in our willingness to embody reconciling action that serves the needs of the world. An awareness of injustice, a willingness to forgive, and a commitment to making right relationships in our communities become embodied in practical actions. Without such commitment, the Eucharist is little more than an empty rite.

Conclusion

What *do* we want for ourselves and for our church? This is an important question, for we shape ourselves and our church in the image of what we desire. We need spiritual wisdom that in faith can say: "Blessed are we, for our hearts long for reconciliation and we know we are sanctified through the transforming power of the Holy One who abides in us to do God's work of reconciliation." Then we will have heard the angel's cry.

In his book *No Future without Forgiveness,* Desmond Tutu, with characteristic passion, sets out his credo. I can think of no more appropriate way of ending than by quoting a passage that describes the Christian hope for reconciliation.

There is a movement, not easily discernible, at the heart of things to reverse the awful centrifugal force of alienation, brokenness, division, hostility and disharmony. God has set in motion a centripetal process, a moving toward the Centre, towards unity, harmony, goodness, peace and justice; one that removes barriers. Jesus says, "And when I am lifted up from the earth I shall draw everyone to myself," as he hangs from His cross with out-flung arms, thrown out to clasp all, everyone and everything, in cosmic embrace, so that all, everyone, everything, belongs. None is an outsider, all are insiders, all belong. There are no aliens; all belong in one family, God's family, and the human family.[9]

Notes

1. Flora A. Keshgegian, *Redeeming Memories: A Theology of Healing and Transformation* (Nashville: Abingdon, 2000), 195.

2. Quoted from Herman Wiersinga, *Verzoening als Verandering: Een gegeven voor menselijk handelen* (Baarn: Bosch & Keuning, 1972), 18. Original text reads: "Deze vraag zie ik als het echte atheïsme. Wie zo'n vraag stelt, wie gelooft dat de mens niet veranderen kan, die gelooft écht niet in God. In die bijbel heet wat wij 'verandering' noemen immers 'verlossing.'"

3. Keshgegian, *Redeeming Memories*, 195.

4. See Donald W. Shriver, *An Ethic for Enemies: Forgiveness in Politics* (New York: Oxford University Press, 1995), 6–9.

5. L. Gregory Jones, *Embodying Forgiveness: A Theological Analysis* (Grand Rapids: Eerdmans, 1995), 184.

6. Robert J. Schreiter, *The Ministry of Reconciliation: Spirituality and Strategies* (Maryknoll, N.Y.: Orbis, 1998), 58.

7. Thomas Merton, *New Seeds of Contemplation* (London: Burns & Oates, 2002), 49.

8. Thomas Merton, *Thoughts on Solitude* (New York: Farrar, Straus & Giroux, 1988), 74.

9. Desmond M. Tutu, *No Future without Forgiveness* (London: Rider, 1999), 213.

Love in a Culture of Fear

Margaret R. Miles

God was in Christ reconciling the world to himself.

(2 CORINTHIANS 5:19)

T HE MOST REVEREND Frank T. Griswold, Presiding Bishop and Primate of the Episcopal Church, USA, whose work we honor in this volume, has said that "the mission of the church is to participate in God's mission." That mission is reconciliation of the world God *so loved.* Often, reconciliation is thought of as abolishing differences. Indeed, urgent injunctions to unity throughout the history of Christianity have resulted repeatedly in the exclusion of differences of belief and practice. Yet God's work in the world cannot be the eradication of difference, but rather the extension of God's love to and within the world's full complexity and particularity.

There are, however, energies at work in our society that can block our participation in God's rich and generous love. One of the most prominent of these is fear. People, whose vulnerable bodies are always subject to disease and accident, have always had much to fear.

But we have not always lived in societies in which fear was actively cultivated and often exaggerated. And living in a culture of fear makes it difficult to live in passionate, generous, and loving engagement in our needy world.

Several Western authors have suggested that human beings and societies can be *defined* by their love or their fear. In his *Enchiridion*, the fifth-century African, Augustine of Hippo, said, "If you wish to know who a person is, ask what he loves." Centuries later, Sigmund Freud suggested that to understand a person, one must ask what she fears. Two thousand years before Franklin D. Roosevelt asserted that "fear itself" should be feared for its capacity to undermine human well-being, the author of the New Testament book of First John described the relationship of love and fear. "Perfect love," he said, "casts out fear" (1 John 4:16). Interpreting this text for his congregation, Augustine said that God *is* love and when Christians love generously, freely, and without self-interest, we *are* God's body in the world. I will first describe some features of the culture of fear in which we live and its effects; then I will offer some suggestions for living lovingly, as God's body, in this context.

A Culture of Fear

In the last several years American daily newspapers, newscasts, and news magazines have featured many causes for fear, some of them grossly exaggerated in terms of the actual danger they represent. Isolated incidents are regularly characterized as trends, and anecdotes are substituted for facts. Moreover, since fear factors do not capture our imaginations for long, new reasons to fear are continually discovered. Remember Y2K? Killer bees, razor blades in Halloween candy, killer kids, road rage, anthrax, mad cow disease, homelessness, computer viruses, homicide rates, and even AIDS have now largely yielded front-page space to terrorism.

In his book *The Culture of Fear,* Barry Glassner pointed out that Americans fear the wrong things. For example, in 2001, over 42,000 Americans were killed in motor vehicle accidents, while 3,547 people were killed *worldwide* in terrorist attacks, 3,000 of them on September 11.[1] But traffic deaths are not news, except when celebrities are involved. More subtle anxieties are also a part of the steady diet of fear we consume every day: fear of flying, harmful foods, fat, aging . . . the list could go on and on. The point is *not* that there is no reason to fear, but that the *culture* of fear in which we live takes our attentions and energies away from creatively addressing the pressing problems of American society, instead encouraging attitudes of helplessness—or worse, aggression.

Who benefits from the culture of fear? The most obvious beneficiaries are TV stations, news magazines and news programs, advocacy groups that sell memberships, lawyers selling class-action lawsuits, and elected officials. According to political commentator Joseba Zulaika, the tragic events of September 11, 2001 "transformed a president whose election had been the most questioned ever into a president with the highest popularity ever."[2] And Jonathan Alter wrote in *Newsweek* that the subtext of President Bush's advertising campaign for the 2004 election was very clear, namely that "We should be afraid, very afraid, for our physical safety should he lose."[3] More generally, fear prompts consumption. As

Michael Moore observed, "Keep everyone afraid, and they'll consume," in order to feel better temporarily.

We must also ask, who suffers from a culture of fear? The answer is, everyone, but some more than others. Fear is hard on bodies. According to Glassner, anxiety is the number one health problem in the country, leading to epidemic depression, alcoholism, eating disorders, and prescription drug addiction. In a culture of contagious insecurity, psychological vulnerability makes Americans willing to live in gated communities and to lose civil liberties and privacy in exchange for security measures.[4]

Moreover, American society is violent because it is fearful.[5] Americans incarcerate at 14 times the rate of Japan, 8 times the rate of France, and 6 times the rate of Canada.[6] The Bureau of Justice Statistics reports that executions in the United States rose from zero in 1969 to 98 in 1999. On the global level, evidence suggesting that counterterrorism activities provoke more terrorism has not been taken seriously, and Americans have become willing to accept proposals for pre-emptive strikes. It is startling that the wealthiest society in the world does not feed its needy young, care for the old and the sick, and assist the poor to earn a living wage. In fact, collective neglect of those who are vulnerable is the norm.

Marc and Marque-Luisa Miringoff's 1999 book *The Social Health of the Nation: How America Is Really Doing* argues that while Americans receive constant reports on the nation's economic health, reports on the nation's social health are few and episodic. Social health is measured by assessing such factors as "the well-being of America's children and youth, the accessibility of health care, the quality of education, the adequacy of housing, the security and satisfaction of work, and the nation's sense of community, citizenship, and diversity."[7] Yet reports on these factors are not publicly and regularly available as part of our picture of "how we're doing" as a society. If social data were regularly reported, the Miringoffs say, Americans would have to acknowledge that despite a booming economy, several key social indicators have worsened significantly over time and are currently performing at levels far below what was achieved in previous decades.

> Suicide rates among the young are 36% higher than they were in 1970. . . . Income inequality is at its third worst level in 50 years. More than 41 million Americans are without health insurance, the worst performance since records have been kept. Violent crime remains almost double what it was in 1970. . . . Average wages for American workers have fallen sharply since the early 1970s, despite the strong economy. Child abuse has increased dramatically. . . . Approximately one in every five children in America today lives in poverty, a 33% increase since 1970.[8]

Since 1970, the gross domestic product has risen 140 percent, but America's social health has decreased by 38 percent. When these figures are compared in the same categories with other industrialized nations, it is evident that Americans are not doing all we can to improve our social health. For example, although the infant mortality rate improved steadily throughout the twentieth century, twenty industrial nations have fewer infant deaths (per 1000 live births) than the United States. Moreover, infant mortality rates vary significantly by race; the rate among African Americans is "more than twice as high as the white rates, a proportional gap that is higher than the one in 1970."[9]

A constructed culture of fear paralyzes Americans' ability to address systemically the evils of poverty, hunger, desperation, and violent aggression in our homes, on our streets, and across the globe, persuading us that any effort is doomed to failure. We must discover practical ways to confront the rhetoric by which fear is established as a way of life. I suggest that the passive, "helpless victim" mentality and aggression resulting from fear can be challenged by a committed *practice* of love.

Making a Loving Society

"Love," in North American media culture, is a much overused and abused word. Romantic love is the subject of most of our television and movie dramas. And we employ the word for even our most trivial fondnesses: "I love animals," one wit has said, "I think they're delicious." Rather than attempting to define love, let us for the moment accept Augustine's insistence that love is not primarily a state of mind or emotions, but an *activity*. He said: "Love has feet . . . love has hands, which give to the poor, love has eyes, which give information about who is in need, love has ears. . . . To see love's *activity* is to see God."[10] Love is not a state one falls into passively, as usually represented in American media. It is something individuals and societies actively *make*. Christians are exhorted to *make* love. Love is not, in the words of the twentieth-century poet e. e. cummings,

"Words, words, as if all worlds were there." In short, love is not rhetoric, but a practice of daily life.

If love has the potential of eliminating fear, however, fear can also disable love. I suggest that the rhetoric of romantic love in our entertainment culture effectively functions as "misdirection," a magician's term for the dramatic gesture that attracts attention in order to prevent spectators from noticing what the magician is doing with his *other* hand. Our society's preoccupation with romantic love takes our attention away from noticing that loving treatment of needy human beings, in the form of social services, health care, and support for education, is disappearing.

The 2004 Mel Gibson movie, *The Passion of the Christ*, can be seen as another example of misdirection. In the context of a society that is becoming meaner and meaner to the vulnerable, the movie invites spectators to contemplate the sufferings of Christ. Its focus on the last hours of Jesus' life erases most of his life and teachings. If attention were directed to his life and actions, instead of on what was done *to* him, a very different picture of Christ's mission would appear. For, according to the Gospels, Jesus spent his adult life healing sick bodies and feeding people, as well as teaching them. In the context of a society in which tax cuts ensure the wealth of the rich and the poverty of the poor, however, to claim that Jesus' life and work stood for the kind of compassion that would establish a more equitable distribution of resources may not be the basis for a box office success.

Living lovingly in a culture of fear requires attention and intention. If Americans are effectively to confront our culture of fear with a practice of love, we must have resources. Many Americans of diverse religious commitments find in their religious convictions motivation and energy for working for social justice, ecological responsibility, and political engagement. A disciplined attentiveness to beauty in its myriad forms is also a vast resource. But it must be acknowledged that spirituality, the secular religion of our time, can also be used to escape these tasks.

The daily practice of love requires that we live with our uncertainties rather than catering to them. As human beings with limited knowledge and perspectives, we are always uncertain, even about the most crucial matters. We do not know the generously responsible way to address particular situations. We always pursue the common good in the dark *by faith*, not knowing for sure what it looks like or feels like; sometimes we do not even recognize it when we see it. However, fear that we do not possess certain knowledge of the humanly good must not be allowed to prevent our passionate commitment to it.[11]

The dominant religious and intellectual traditions of the West seem to have neglected the urgencies of this world in favor of attention to another world, of ideas or values. Until the second half of the twentieth century, it was not possible to identify and map with scientific precision the interconnectedness of living beings. A few Western and Eastern philosophers intuited an interdependent web of sentient beings, but those intuitions could not be documented, so those who subscribed to them were labeled "romantic," "soft," or "nature-worshipers" by "hard-headed" philosophers. But now, the tangible effects of environmental crises such as the disappearance of the rain forests, the extinction of animal species, and pollution of air, food, and water can be measured. The fundamental fact of life is that the universe is utterly interdependent. This knowledge is no longer intuited or romantic, but factual and concrete. As the novelist Maxine Hong Kingston put it, "There is already an amazing gold ring connecting every living being as surely as if we held hands, flippers and paws, feelers and wings."[12]

Christianity, like other world religions, has traditionally been very concerned about the danger of attachment to power and possessions, but the equal dangers of resignation, passivity, cynicism, and indifference to the suffering and struggling of other living beings have not been articulated as frequently or as forcefully. Similarly, Christians often emphasize the power and greatness of God in ways that de-emphasize human responsibility. Theologies that focus on humans' child-like dependence on God can fail to challenge Christians to mature activity and accountability. The feminist philosopher Dorothy Dinnerstein wrote, "We never feel as grown-up as we expected to feel when we were children."[13] Because we do not always, or perhaps often, feel confident and capable, we evade responsibility. Yet *we are* the grownups. No spirituality should help us transcend the needy world in which we live, a world that requires our attention, affection, and most of all, our *work.*

A practice of love for the twenty-first century can be exercised in many arenas—in politics, from voting to running for public office; in ecological activity—from recycling to advocacy; in social justice—from awareness of who suffers to support for proposals for relief. We must resist being overwhelmed by the multiplicity of dangers facing us. Since one individual cannot work effectively on all urgent matters, each of us must take the risk and responsibility of deciding how to focus our efforts without requiring that everyone focus on the same projects. Indeed, I must be grateful that others are correcting the one-sidedness of my vision by addressing problems and dangers that my experience has not prepared me to detect.[14]

Finally, as Augustine said, "We are the times; if we are good, the times are good," or, in contemporary parlance, "the times R us."[15] We can resist the rhetoric of fear that surrounds us, intentionally and actively replacing it with a practice of love. We can insist on defining ourselves not by our fear, but by our loving active concern for the beautiful world in which we live and for the consummate, irreducible, and irreplaceable *worth* of all living beings. The 1983 Peace Ribbon project took a similar approach. Rather than focus on the horrific effects of nuclear war, panels of the banner depicted what its creators valued most dearly. The fifteen-mile-long banner, wound several times around the Pentagon and the Capitol Building in Washington, D.C., bore images of fruit and flowers, trees, ocean, loved faces, dancing figures, and lines of poetry and scripture.

The effects of fear are today more evident than ever in history, but to work to create a loving society is to participate in God's mission of reconciling the world to Godself. It is to be God's body in the world. Let us resolve to place our attention and energies not on the rhetoric of fear that surrounds us, but on the practices of love.

Notes

1. Barry Glassner, *The Culture of Fear: Why Americans Are Afraid of the Wrong Things* (New York: Basic Books, 1999), xvii.

2. Joseba Zulaika, "The Self-Fulfilling Prophecies of Counter-terrorism," *Radical History* 85 (Winter 2003): 194.

3. Jonathan Alter, "The Fight for High Ground," *Newsweek* (March 15, 2004), 42.

4. Glassner, *Culture of Fear,* 162; see also Jeffrey Rosen, *The Naked Crowd: Reclaiming Security and Freedom in an Anxious Age* (New York: Random House, 2004).

5. Larissa MacFarquhar, "The Populist: Michael Moore's Art and Anger," *The New Yorker* (February 16, 2004), 138.

6. Brent Staples's review of *Life on the Outside, New York Times Book Review* (March 21, 2004), 7.

7. Marque-Luisa Miringoff, Marc Miringoff, and Sandra Opdycke, *The Social Report: Assessing the Progress of America by Monitoring the Well-Being of Its People* (Tarrytown, N.Y.: Fordham Institute for Innovation in Social Policy, 2001), 23–49.

8. Marc Miringoff and Marque-Luisa Miringoff, *The Social Health of the Nation: How America Is Really Doing* (New York: Oxford University Press, 1999), 5.

9. Miringoff and Miringoff, *Social Health,* 50.

10. Augustine, Homily 7.6; *Ten Homilies on the First Epistle of St. John in Augustine's Later Works,* John Burnaby, ed. (Philadelphia: Library of Christian Classics, Westminster Press, 1955).

11. Margaret R. Miles, *Reading for Life: Beauty, Pluralism, and Responsibility* (New York: Continuum, 1997), 202.

12. Maxine Hong Kingston, *China Men* (New York: Knopf, 1980), 92.

13. Dorothy Dinnerstein, *The Mermaid and the Minotaur: Sexual Arrangements and Human Malaise* (New York: Harper & Row, 1976), 190.

14. Margaret R. Miles, *Practicing Christianity: Critical Perspectives for an Embodied Christianity* (New York: Crossroad, 1988), 183.

15. Augustine, *Sermon* 80.8.

Praying in Community: Becoming Our Truest Selves

Michael Battle

C OMMUNITY IS THE ESSENTIAL foundation for Christian spirituality, and an understanding of this reality is crucial for Christian life. Herein is the genius of Presiding Bishop Frank Griswold—namely, his ability to keep individuals focused on acting and being Christian community. Serving as one of his chaplains to the House of Bishops, I learned from Bishop Griswold's deep wisdom concerning communal spirituality. Under his leadership, concepts such as "a community of wisdom" and "reconciliation" came alive and set an expectation for how Christian leadership flourishes.

At a time when few major Christian leaders have taught that the goal of Christian spirituality goes beyond individual fulfillment, Bishop Griswold has shown us that acting like and being a Christian are based on common prayer. As well, he has made plain that common prayer does not diminish personal piety; rather it provides a needed reference point. In this essay, I will explore the notion of how what we practice in common makes us better individuals.

Some may find this emphasis on common prayer

difficult, saying that Scripture teaches us about the need to pray alone. Remember though that when Jesus went alone to pray, Elijah would suddenly appear, or an angel would minister to Jesus. When Jesus went into his closet, shut the door and prayed, there would always be a crowded room: a communion of saints. We often forget this. So, when Jesus instructs us to go into our rooms, shut the door and pray to our Father who is in secret (Matt. 6:6), he is giving a corporate imperative. He is still teaching us to pray in concert, not alone.

Jesus teaches us that spirituality is always about being animated by the other. Jesus says, "When you pray, say Our . . . (Matt. 6:9)." He doesn't say, "My." Common prayer points to how the human heart is made perfect when in the other it finds what it is lacking. The Holy Spirit animates our very beings with God's communal life, and we realize we cannot live unto or by ourselves.

God knows what we need before we ask, yet so many of our private prayers seem not to acknowledge this. We pray to God as if to inform God about something God already knows. However, as we corporately acknowledge God's presence and omniscience, our petitions and intercessions take on meaning. When we pray in community, self-understanding increases as we assist one another in focusing on lasting and sustained needs and yearnings rather than on momentary whims and fleeting desires. Thus, common prayer provides a way of seeing who we truly are in our relationships with one another and with God.

In order to explore what I have learned from Bishop Griswold's example, namely that common prayer is essential in becoming a Christian, I would like to look at three possible obstacles to prayer and to reflect upon how prayer in community might create something new. The first is the reality of suffering.

Suffering

Sometimes human suffering is so severe that one cries with St. Teresa of Avila to God, "No wonder your friends are so few, considering how you treat them." African Christian tradition articulates a spirituality capable of containing suffering. Deep in the Christian faith of black Christians is the understanding that suffering can be redemptive because the Creator God won't let death be the last word. Perhaps this is why black churches cannot help but demonstrate their worship communally and kinetically. As the African American spiritual leader Howard Thurman states:

> . . . despite the personal character of suffering, the sufferer can work his way through to community. . . . Sometimes he discovers through the ministry of his own burden a larger comprehension of his fellows, of whose presence he becomes aware in his darkness. They are companions along the way. The significance of this cannot be ignored or passed over. It is one of the consolations offered by the Christian religion in the centrality of the position given to the cross and to the suffering of Jesus Christ.[1]

Through the life of Christ the world knows that innocent people suffer. Their suffering does not diminish our faith in God. In fact, Thurman thinks, "Their presence in the world is a stabilizing factor, a precious ingredient maintaining the delicate balance that prevents humanity from plunging into the abyss."[2]

Bishop Griswold has given us a vision of a human community capable of living with both suffering and God's presence; he shows us that only through human community can we make sense of this. In community we find a mysterious paradox that could be described as robust vulnerability. Such robust vulnerability is grounded in relationships in which persons are able to recognize that their humanity is bound up in the other's humanity and that we are vulnerable in our dependence on the other. I have called such a paradox of community by the name of "Ubuntu."[3]

Invulnerability

Suffering can cause us to harden our souls and embrace stoic tendencies, that is, to become less vulnerable. A sense of invulnerability, however, makes it difficult to pray. For the Christian mystic Simone Weil, any doctrine of prayer must address two kinds of pain. She writes:

> When we talk of the problem of pain we make a distinction between suffering and affliction. The problem of suffering or mere pain is how to bear it. When the crisis is over, as in a bout with a headache, the problem disappears. We have a great capacity to be indifferent to this kind of pain. Affliction, on the other hand, is a kind of suffering which marks you indelibly not merely on the body but on the soul. It is the "mark of slavery," signifying an uprooting, a permanent estrangement.[4]

When you suffer, it is tempting to harden your heart and conclude that life is mechanistic. Hardened in our individualistic worldviews we are further tempted: the next temptation is to oppress others—to see them as machines. We are tempted in this way because we learn to see ourselves as mere machines—soulless objects. Affliction deprives its victims of their personality and makes them into things. Community becomes impossible for them. As Weil concludes, affliction "is indifferent; and it is the coldness of this indifference, a metallic coldness, which freezes all those it touches right to the depths of their souls. They will never find warmth again. They will never believe any more that they are anyone."[5] A life of suffering and becoming afflicted can move one into this state of seeing evil as normative. One can become mechanized, and forget how to pray.

In such a mechanistic reality all that matters is power. Power over others legitimates violence and perpetuates warring identities. Desmond Tutu helps us see that this is a very dangerous existence, in which evil and violence become normative and expected. As Archbishop Tutu explains:

> Then there is the mystery of evil. Why should there arise a Hitler, an Amin—why should there be a holocaust perpetrated by those who appeared to be quite normal human beings, why should apparently decent human beings not be incapable of the horrors of apartheid, why should apparently normal people engage in necklacing [burning people bound to automobile tires]? Why should there be those who are not appalled by a Crossroads, who can carry

out the destruction of a District Six, who can torture to death a fellow human being as part of their normal daily life and return home to embrace their wives and children, to eat birthday cake and be to all intents and purposes normal . . . ?[6]

Without communal prayer there is no incentive to rise above a mechanistic reality because individuals will be incapable of seeing beyond survival. As an individual, I am constantly tempted to see creation as the mere survival of the fittest. In such a reality, my goal of existence is to know myself over and against another. But we cannot know God in this way, and we cannot pray in this way.

In community there is a larger picture of God's presence in the world. Through communal prayer the wound of creation is slowly transfigured toward a new heaven and earth. Communal prayer moves us beyond a survivalist religion in which the goal is only self-interest. Another dynamic, which I will only mention here, is that in situations of privilege and an accompanying sense of invulnerability, many fall into individualistic ways of living where achieving one's own best interest is the goal.

Unanswered Prayer

Any discussion of prayer that seems to be unanswered must address the problem of theodicy, namely: Why does God's good creation remain *de facto* violent and capricious? What does the apparently inevitable breakdown of human systems or community say about the presence or absence of God? For example, when Job prays to God for providence in dealing with creation's tragedy and violence, there seems to be no answer for him. Job says, "O that I might have my request, and that God would grant my desire . . . (Job 6:8)." Job is left with unanswered prayer. Here again, Simone Weil provides an insight into how prayer is ultimately answered:

> The key to a Christian conception of studies is the realization that prayer consists of attention. It is the orientation of all the attention of which the soul is capable toward God. The quality of the attention counts for much in the quality of the prayer. Warmth of heart cannot make up for it. The highest part of the attention only makes contact with God, when prayer is intense and pure enough for such a contact to be established; but the whole attention is turned toward God.[7]

Our ability to maintain the fixed attitude of "attention" depends not on successfully penetrating God as on being penetrated by God. As Romans 8 teaches us, it is God who truly prays. According to St. Paul, we do not know how to pray apart from the Spirit praying in us (Rom. 8:26–28). What we actually do when we pray is simply become attentive to the prayer already going on within us.

The Holy Spirit who prays in us, for us, around us, and despite us performs the marvelous miracle of making community possible in a world bent on destruction and chaos. The Holy Spirit's community is about love— a "love," which for Simone Weil was "not a state but a direction" out of chaos.[8] Crucial to practicing common prayer is the spiritual practice of moving in the direction of the Holy Spirit who prays in us such that we participate in the Spirit's ongoing prayer. Like toddlers, we must learn how to talk to God by listening first to God's speech that is constantly uttered in Christian communities, otherwise known as the church.

A community of prayer does not expect a salvation wrought by human hands; rather, it pays attention to what and who is already there, knowing it does not reach goodness of its own accord. A community of prayer knows that it is often only after long, seemingly fruitless effort, when it despairs at prayer being answered, that answered prayer comes as a gift and marvelous surprise. It is through these efforts of attending to God through prayer that we participate in the profound effects of prayer.

Praying in community not only helps remove these obstacles to prayer, it also can move us in counterintuitive directions. For example, when facing a natural inclination to respond with violence, we may rather wait and be patient and nonviolent. When faced with difficult decisions, the appropriate response may be to seek out someone with an ability to discern greater than our own. Suffering and the consequent push toward invulnerability need not make us hunker down in individualistic approaches to God.

Our attentiveness when we pray in common to God's ongoing presence—despite all obstacles—does not make us naïve Christians, as some might have us believe. Why? Because in our attentiveness to the other (the greatest Other being God), we learn to produce that which is greater than our individual parts—community. In other words, as a community of prayer becomes more attentive to God, they move beyond their individual suffering, the attendant push to become invulnerable and the sense that God may not be listening. Common prayer gives us the ability to imagine peaceful governments and a cessation of disease and poverty. Common prayer becomes its own self-fulfilling prophecy. When we pray we destroy the false sense of individual fullness by acknowledging our common need for God. When we pray in common, we accentuate our differences in such a way that we realize that we need each other to know God. Most of all, in common prayer we acknowledge that we are not the ultimate being: God is. This acknowledgment helps us recognize that we are not praying to God as some kind of Santa Claus who grants our every wish.

Each of us has times when prayer is difficult. Communal prayer provides a way for us to pray even when we are unable to pray alone. Then, we can depend on the community to offer intercessory prayer on our behalf.

Training to pray as community provides the necessary reference point for us to honestly and truly know our deepest selves. Communal prayer affirms our uniqueness as persons. Our vocations are made sense of in community. Our talents and gifts function through relationships with others. We need others to know ourselves. And most of all, we need God made known in Jesus to know who we truly are.

Perhaps it is part of the paradoxical nature of life as we experience it that in community individuals become who they truly are called to be. As we become more of a person in God, we experience a divine socialization process that transforms us. I believe that through common prayer, God is working in the world, helping it, and us, to know we are more than animals, more than individuals who have a bundle of rights and privileges. Through our common prayer, with God's help, we can grow in divinity, growing ever more into the image of God.

Notes

1. Walter Earl Fluker et al., eds., *A Strange Freedom: The Best of Howard Thurman on Religious Experience and Public Life* (Boston: Beacon Press, 1998), 47.

2. Fluker, 49.

3. See Michael Battle, *Reconciliation: The Ubuntu Theology of Desmond Tutu* (Cleveland: The Pilgrim Press, 1997).

4. Quoted by E. W. F. Tomlin, *Simone Weil* (Cambridge: Bowes & Bowes, 1954), in the Series Studies in Modern European Literature and Thought, 49.

5. Ibid.

6. Tutu's Handwritten Sermons, "The Angels," St. Michael's Observatory, 1986.

7. Weil, "Reflections on the Right Use of School Studies with a View to the Love of God," in *Simone Weil Reader.* George A. Panichas, ed., (Mt. Kisco, N.Y.: Moyer Bell Ltd., 1977), 44.

8. Weil, *Waiting on God,* 77.

Engaging Friendship as a
Christian Value in Philippians

Cynthia Briggs Kittredge

T HE WRITING AND PREACHING of Frank Griswold
show his theological leadership shaped by the
spirit of Paul's epistles. Stressing the drama of Paul's
conversion and the radical transformation of baptism
and urging concern for the whole body of Christ, Bishop
Griswold's pastoral writing is dyed in the colors and
imagery of Paul's letters. It is with deep appreciation
for his wisdom and courage throughout the tumultuous
living of these days that I offer this essay in his honor.

Scripture gives us access to the experience of our
foreparents in faith. Even with all the complications of
translation, the language of the Bible communicates the
way in which Christian believers expressed their life in
Christ and the language that gave them life. Throughout
its history the church has saved and passed on these stan-
zas, retold, respoken, and resung them in different keys.
Through proclaiming this language in their own tongue,
the church has sought in Scripture new life-giving visions amid competing narratives in its culture. Reading
Scripture has guided ethical decision-making, the orga-
nizing of communities, and the forming of relationships.

Like the Gospel of John, from which the title *I Have Called You Friends* is taken, the letters of Paul convey the deep concern for the character of relationships among believers and how those relationships formed the community, or what the text calls the *ecclesia*, "assembly." The writers of the gospels depict their intention that their communities reflect the teaching of Jesus. When Jesus called his followers "friends" (*philoi*) he was inviting them into a renewed relationship with one another and with himself that was mutual, intimate, and self-giving. Paul's letters indicate that the efforts of the ecclesia to determine how relationships with each other and with their leaders would be structured were complicated, disputed, and at times very conflicted. Critical reading of the New Testament letters gives us a glimpse into those quarrelsome times and their sometimes uneasy resolution. While Paul's letters do not employ the same word for "friend" as John, the values of friendship emerge as a defining mark of the ecclesia shared by Paul and the congregations. Friendship has not been a prominent theme in the history of interpretation of Paul, but when sought out, explored, and engaged in Scripture, friendship invites a view of relationship and an alternative vision for community that challenges many of the most dominant models in our culture. Of all of Paul's letters, Philippians is most saturated with the language of friendship and will be the focus of this exploration.

Every interpreter comes to the reading of Paul's letters with distinct ideas about who Paul was and what the early assemblies were like. In looking to the letters for a life-giving vision, readers make choices within the canon of Paul's letters about what texts, images, and themes to emphasize and proclaim. To be explicit about the choices one makes as a reader is one of the principles of the ethics of interpretation. When I read Paul's letters, the commitment that shapes my interpretation is that the members of the ecclesia knew the reality and conviction of the gospel of Jesus Christ through its corporate reading of Scripture and its sacramental worship. Through the experience of the Spirit sisters and brothers in the ecclesia shared access to power that bestowed gifts for leadership upon them. Because of this fundamentally corporate character of the gospel, the primary aim of interpreting the letters of Paul is to appreciate and reconstruct the communities in their fullness and diversity rather than only Paul's views as a single authoritative individual. Then as readers in contemporary communities, we can spiritually engage with those forebears and their faithful wrestling with the gospel.

Written to the congregation at Philippi while Paul was in prison, the letter to the Philippians is distinctive among the letters of Paul for the emotional language used to address the recipients and the many references to the warm relationship between Paul and the congregation.[1] The opening thanksgiving of the letter recalls the past history between Paul and the congregation:

> I thank my God every time I remember you,
> constantly praying with joy in every one of my
> prayers for all of you, because of your sharing in
> the gospel from the first day until now.[2]

The word translated as "sharing" is the word *koinonia*, which could also be translated as "communion" or "partnership." Paul uses emotional words, which are conventionally used in letters of friendship:

It is right for me to think this way about all of
you, because you hold me in your heart, for all
of you share in God's grace with me, both in
my imprisonment and in the defense and confirmation of the gospel. For God is my witness,
how I long for all of you with the compassion of
Christ Jesus.[3]

The English phrase "for all of you share" is expressed
in one Greek word, *sugkoinonous,* which combines the
preposition "with" with the same root, *koinonia.* The
opening of the letter emphasizes the longing of Paul to
be with them, the importance of their mutual prayers
for one another in Paul's imprisonment, and their common struggle for the gospel (1:30). The relationship, the
partnership, is the focus of the letter. By strengthening the bonds of their friendship, Paul urges them to
continue to act in accordance with the gospel as they
understand it:

Only, live your life in a manner worthy of the
gospel of Christ, so that, whether I come and
see you or am absent and hear about you, I will
know that you are standing firm in one spirit,
striving side by side with one mind for the faith
of the gospel. . . .[4]

"Striving side by side" is translated from another compound of the preposition *sun,* "with": *sunathlountes,* "co-
athletes." The stress on being of one mind is another
typical feature of friendship language. At the end of
the letter this vocabulary of sharing recurs when Paul
speaks of the congregation "sharing," *sugkoinonesantes,*

in his distress (4:14). Paul speaks of a distinctive aspect of his relationship with the Philippian church:

> You Philippians indeed know that in the early days of the gospel, when I left Macedonia, no church shared with me (*ekoinonesen*) in the matter of giving and receiving, except you alone. For even when I was in Thessalonica, you sent me help for my needs more than once.[5]

The partnership is enacted by means of financial gifts. Paul's language here stresses the mutual benefit of the gift and the fact that it is offered as a fragrant offering and a sacrifice to God. Paul stresses the mutuality of the "giving and receiving" in order to assure that the giving of a gift does not, as it might have in that cultural context, place them in a relationship of asymmetrical obligation or inequality.[6]

Each of Paul's letters employs the language and traditions of the church to whom he writes. In the case of Philippians, the prominence of this vocabulary of sharing, communion, partnership, or friendship indicates that this community especially prized this value.

In order to encourage his friends in Philippi to live their lives in a manner worthy of the gospel, Paul uses the rhetorical technique of giving examples or "proofs" to illustrate this shared value. The first and most important positive proof is the "Christ hymn" of Philippians 2:6–11. The hymn is introduced by an exhortation to "be of the same mind, having the same love, being in full accord and of one mind," the ideals of friendship. Continuing to connect with his audience, Paul quotes this poetic tradition, well known to the congregation as a piece they have often sung in the context of their worship to celebrate the resurrection of Jesus. In this tradition, structured in two movements, of descent and ascent, Christ renounces his status as one in the form of God to take on the status of a slave. In response to this act of self-emptying, God raises Jesus to the position of God and gives him the name of "Lord." Although the emphasis of the tradition may have originally been on the second half of the hymn, the ascent, Paul gives special attention to the first half, the descent, in order to urge selflessness and humility upon the congregation.

The second positive example is Paul's commendation of Epaphroditus and Timothy, both of whom exemplify those who look after the interests of others above their own. Paul says that Timothy will be "genuinely concerned for your welfare" and that Epaphroditus cares for the emotions of the congregation. Timothy is likened to a "son with a father" (2:22) and Epaphroditus is called a "brother and co-worker and fellow soldier" (2:25). Epaphroditus closely resembles Paul, being close to death and putting himself at risk on behalf of others in order to deliver monetary gifts from Philippi (4:18). Paul cites himself as the final positive example of the behavior he urges when he describes himself in 3:4–11 as having given up privilege and gain for the sake of Jesus Christ. He contrasts his own positive example with a negative example: "Beware of the dogs, beware of the evil workers, beware of those who mutilate the flesh!" These he describes in 3:18 as "enemies of the cross of Christ." Christ, Epaphroditus, Paul, and Timothy all represent those who renounce privilege in order to look not to their own interests but to the interests of others (2:4).

Following the series of proofs, Paul directly addresses

two individuals by name, Euodia and Syntyche, whom he entreats to "be of the same mind in the Lord." He asks another individual, whom he calls "my loyal companion," to assist them. The phrase "loyal companion" (*gnesie syzyge*), may also be translated as "one who is truly yoked." Words for shared work in the gospel are concentrated here: Euodia and Syntyche have "co-contested" (*sunathlesen*) with Paul along with Clement and other "fellow workers" (*sunergoi*). Nothing is definitively known about the identity of these two ministers with evocative names (Euodia means "good way" and Syntyche "fortunate") or about the nature of the dispute that led Paul to urge them to "be of one mind." The enigmatically described *gnesie syzyge* may be a kind of antitype to the two who are in Paul's perspective not thoroughly "yoked." Different historical reconstructions of the situation that gave rise to this entreaty reveal various interpretive assumptions about the nature of ministry and leadership in the ecclesia. Most important to observe is the extensive use of words describing partnership in the service of the gospel, and the implication that "yoking," collaborative working, is the image for positive relationships.

In using the language of oneness, affection, and common effort for a shared cause, Paul is drawing on the conventional vocabulary and patterns of ancient Greek friendship.[7] Unlike modern ideas of personal friendship, in the writings of Greco-Roman moralists, friendship is an ideal relationship with the purpose of moral instruction. A basic obligation of friendship was giving and receiving. The norm for ideal friendship was the relationship among aristocratic men of equal social status, but in exceptional circumstances friendship could be made between a person of high status and one of lower rank. In the dramatic logic of Philippians, there is parallelism between the friendship between Paul and the Philippians, the Philippians and one another, and the friendship they each have with Christ, the one in the form of God who took on the form of a slave. Another distinctive aspect of the ancient ideal of friendship was its dialectical relationship with the idea of enmity. Friends shared common enemies, and invective against shared foes was part of the relationship-strengthening rhetoric of friendship. The letter to the Philippians constructs enemies as negative examples as well as friends as positive models. Paul makes an implied contrast between friends and enemies in 1:15–16:

> Some proclaim Christ from envy and rivalry, but others from goodwill. These proclaim Christ out of love, knowing that I have been put here for the defense of the gospel; the others proclaim Christ out of selfish ambition, not sincerely but intending to increase my suffering in my imprisonment.

Expressions of intense affection for friends are juxtaposed with harsh language against the enemies of the cross of Christ in 3:18. Interpreting friendship in Philippians requires taking into account both kinds of rhetoric and being aware of other ambiguities as well. For Christian people and pastors to conceive of life-giving visions from these texts, one must grapple with the tensions built into the biblical rhetoric. One challenge is the dialectical relationship between friendship and enmity in its expression in Philippians. Paul strengthens allegiance to gospel values shared by the Christian friends by intensifying the polemics against "the enemies of the cross of Christ." As affectionate as is the address to friends, is the harshness of the invective against those who are enemies. So abrupt is the transition of tone between the note of rejoicing in 3:1 and the severe warning in 3:2 that some scholars have identified the harsh attack as a fragment of another letter. In religious and political rhetoric, exaggerating the vices and the dangers of "outsiders" in order to strengthen bonds within a community has a long and violent history. Castigating one's enemies with the eloquence that Paul does exacts a very high price and puts the friendship paradigm at risk. Theologians must critically engage this dimension of the scriptural texts.

Another ambiguous feature of the language of friendship in Philippians is the tension between the mutuality that defines friendship and the hierarchy inherent in other models, particularly the master/slave image and the father/son image. The hierarchically structured relationships occur in the language of obeying in 2:12 and in Paul's designation of Timothy: "as a son with a father he served me in the gospel." When Paul uses this kind of language he subtly asserts his own dominance in the community despite the presence of other leaders.

Finally, in his rhetoric of unity in Philippians, Paul comes close to equating "unity" with agreement with and obedience to him. This rhetorical technique too still operates in a disguised fashion in our ecclesiological and ecumenical relationships. Scripture's rhetoric can give life-giving warning as well as affirmation.

It is natural that readers of the letter throughout the history of its interpretation have attributed the theological development of the value of friendship to the writer of the letter, Paul. Paul's frequent references to the importance of his own presence and example for maintaining behavior worthy of the gospel make Paul the central focus of attention. However, because of the relational nature of friendship and because of the effort made by the author to appeal to this value, it is more correct to emphasize that friendship was a value of the gospel community, shared by all. As we know from the baptismal creeds from other letters and the consequential moral exhortation, the experience of baptism into Christ's death and resurrection established this new creation where the baptized became children of God or, in a different key, became "friends" of one another (Gal. 3:27–29; 1 Cor. 12:12–13; Col. 3:11). At the opening of the letter, Paul addresses all in the community "to all the saints in Christ Jesus who are in Philippi, with the bishops (*episcopoi*) and deacons (*diaconoi*) among them." He commends Timothy, Epaphroditus, Euodia, Syntyche, and Clement by name and sends greetings from "the sisters and brothers" in 4:21.[8] These references indicate the presence of ongoing leadership in the community at Philippi. These Christ believers would have been reading Scripture, retelling the story of Jesus' death in the baptism and eucharist, and living out the moral implications of the Christ hymn in their life in the ecclesia. Paul's letters and perhaps letters from and among other Christians offered them means of strengthening their shared values and developing moral instruction.

The strong stress upon friendship in Philippians and the importance of others who are in "partnership" (*koinonia*) with Paul draws attention to the many commendations of co-workers throughout the letters, notably Phoebe, described as "sister," "deacon," "bene-factor" (Rom. 16:1–2), Prisca and Aquila (Rom. 16:3), and Andronicus and Junia "prominent among the apostles" (Rom. 16:7). Many co-workers with Paul are described with various titles and epithets, and later interpreters have tried to correlate these terms with later ministerial "offices." However, when these terms are read in light of the language friendship in Philippians, then all these roles can be understood as vigorous collaboration in the same gospel enterprise.

Adapted from Greco-Roman ideals of friendship and reinforced through the practices of worship and service, the paradigm of friendship in the Christian community offers a life-giving vision to our own communities. The historical and cultural distance between the world of this text and our own world means that it is not possible to simply import or replicate the worldview of the text without critical reflection and adaptation. Rather, the distance gives us a critical angle on our own culture and at the same time offers resources for alternative visions. We read and proclaim this text of our foreparents in a culture where a dominant model of primary relationship is that between seller and buyer, seller and consumer. In the media and in international relations, people and peoples are potential markets, and exhorting others to consume is a major feature of our communication. Value is linked tightly to cost or to price, and worth is evaluated in monetary terms. Relationships of domination and subordination continue to be the norm, and often these continue to be linked with theories of nature and race. In a highly eroticized culture, relationships between women and men are often seen in exclusively romanticized terms.

To this contemporary cultural environment, the values of the gospel community at Philippi present a compelling alternative. It is clear that the partnership of giving and receiving is a mutual one—where each party gives and receives. The relationship is enacted with material, economic exchange as well as a sharing of spiritual gifts. Members of the community have been given new birth by the death and resurrection of Jesus and are bound by a common goal, "striving side by side with one mind for the sake of the gospel." In North American culture, where elevation of social status is a dominant ideal, Philippians exhorts those of high status to renounce privilege for the sake of their "friends." In the letter to the Philippians, it does not appear that male and female gender distinction defines the relationships among Euodia, Syntyche, Paul, Clement, or Epaphroditus. The exception may be Timothy, whose relationship "as a son to a father" does have specific gender connotations. While friendship is a male ideal in Greek philosophical writing, friendship and gospel partnership in Philippians include women and men. John's gospel too, with its central women characters: Mary Magdalene, Mary and Martha of Bethany, and the Samaritan woman, indicates that the *philoi* of Jesus were female and male. The model of non-sexualized friendship between Christian women and men is a counter-cultural vision within our current sexualized climate.

As pastors, teachers, leaders, and kin in Christ, we interpret and proclaim Scripture today in the midst of complex and passionate disputes over ideals of Christian relationship and models of church structure as intense as those arguments that appear among the New Testament epistles. These ideals and models originate in and draw their power from the scriptural texts from which they have been elaborated. Searching out and exploring the paradigm of friendship, so valued by the Philippian church, theologically and christologically explored in Paul's letter from prison, and liturgically celebrated in the Christ hymn, open up a model of mutuality and self-giving intimacy that challenges the strongest values of our secular culture and even of some prominent conventions of our church life. Aware of the tensions within the ancient and modern rhetoric of friendship, we can exercise care in our preaching and mutual moral exhortation in such a way that an exaggerated language of enmity does not endanger the principle of friendship we hold. As did the congregation at Philippi, we can continue to think through and to practice together what it means to share partnership in the gospel.

Notes

1. For detailed analysis see Kittredge, *Community and Authority: The Rhetoric of Obedience in the Pauline Tradition* (Harrisburg, Pa.: Trinity Press International, 1998).

2. Phil. 1:3–5. Bible translations are from the NRSV unless otherwise noted.

3. Phil. 1:7–8.

4. Phil. 1:27.

5. Phil. 4:15–16.

6. Steven Fowl, *Interpretation* 56, no. 1 (January 2002): 45–58.

7. See Stanley K. Stowers, "Friends and Enemies in the Politics of Heaven: Reading Theology in Philippians" in Jouette M. Bassler, ed., *Pauline Theology* (Minneapolis: Fortress, 1991), 105–21 and the literature cited there.

8. The NRSV translates *adelphoi* in 4:21 as "friends."

God's Conditional Love: The Inner Work of Reconciliation

Curtis G. Almquist, SSJE

I T WAS LATE AUTUMN of 1986 and I sat in the office of the new Bishop-Coadjutor of Chicago, Frank T. Griswold, tears dripping off my chin. A week earlier I had announced my resignation from a parish of the diocese where I was happily serving, for the purpose of testing a vocation to be a monk, a growing intrigue for me since I was age 12. Though I had felt some joyous clarity in making the decision, that morning I was absolutely desolate and confused. Had I made a terrible mistake? Bishop Griswold listened as I retraced my life, explaining something of how I had come to that moment, and then he responded, speaking to my desolation with great compassion, wisdom, even a little humor. I left him reminded of God's abiding love and consoled in my decision—and that has made all the difference.

During his tenure as our chief pastor and teacher, Bishop Griswold has consistently spoken of reconciliation as the primary concern for Christians: personal, ecclesial, and global reconciliation. In this essay I speak about personal reconciliation, a theme ever-present in spiritual direction. Spiritual direction—companioning others in their journey to Christ—has been a primary ministry practiced by my own monastic community since our founding in the 1860s.

Spiritual direction for our future is informed by spiritual reconciliation with our past. Who we are, what we are, however it is we've gotten to be where we are, God knows, God lures, God loves. I would call this God's "conditional love." Life is inescapably full of conditions and circumstances, changes and chances, and God's love for us is there and present in it all. It is not simply an idea but a living reality. God's love for us is real and personal, woven into the very fabric of our lives from the very beginning. God's love is woven through what has happened to us, and what has not happened: the parents to whom we were born; whether we were desired by them; whether they stayed together; whether they had enough money, or space, or time, or patience, whether or how they praised and raised us; how their love for us was informed by their needs and desires and confusions; whether our upbringing was an experience of liberation or a sentence of incarceration. God's love is mediated through our siblings, or the absence of siblings, through our teachers, coaches, pastors, relatives, neighbors, co-workers, and friends. They all have shared in our formation or, perhaps in some tragic ways, in our *de*formation. Whether we learned about courage, shame, joy, perseverance, fear, or patience, even from our earliest days, has been very much informed by the conditions in which we were raised.

God's love for us is known in our experience of joy and forgiveness, of sickness and health, of acclamation and success, of justice and cruelty, of favoritism and desire, of altruism and discrimination, in our experience of what is dependably old and what is excitingly new, in the tiniest and in the greatest of ways. God's love is present in our searching for a home or dwelling place, of discovering *that* we belong, or *where* we belong, or *if* we belong. God's love is for us is known in the experience of finding our voice, or losing our voice, and in our occasions to travel into worlds otherwise unknown. *These* are the conditions in which we experience life, and through which we must survive and thrive. These are the conditions of life, oftentimes less than ideal. But that's life.

In these "conditions" we know God's love because of Jesus, who comes to us, stooping low to meet us at our own level. We are loved by Jesus, not despite our history but in light of our history. We are no longer talking only about a God of the Law, whose ways were unknowable, whose face was unseeable, whose name was unpronounceable, whose heart and hands were untouchable. Rather, we see Jesus, who enters the conditions of this world as an innocent and needy child, just as we have, to reveal the real presence of God's love. Emmanuel—God with us—is not only God above us or beyond us, but God *with* us. God with *you* in the conditions and in the relationships in which you have known life, past and present. God loves you. God loves *you*. You are the apple of God's eye.

Unless we are on friendly speaking terms with our own past, we won't be able to recognize God's call into the future. God looks on each of us as a whole person. For most people, this includes a broken past. God is very frugal in this way, wasting nothing in our lives, desiring to make use of it all. People who are searching for God's love and direction do so because something is missing, because something is not right in their life. They search for God *not* because they are so bright, *not* because they are so gifted, or successful, or eloquent. They search for God *not* because they are handsome, disciplined, healthy, or secure. It's *not* because of their glittering image. Their quest to know God's love is because something is broken in their life—something about the conditions of their past or their present that is damaged or incomplete or vacuous. That break is often God's entry point. That break is *God's* break, God's *breakthrough* to them. The gospel tells us that Jesus has come *to seek and to save the lost:* lost childhoods, lost chances, lost hopes, lost relationships, lost needs . . . and to love us back to life.

There's an old adage that says, "Love is blind." That is not true. I think it's quite the opposite. Love is eyes wide open. Love sees beyond the moment, below the surface, deep inside the other, with what could be called insight or mercy, the enlightening of the eyes of the heart. This is the nature of God's love, God's love *for you.* The conditions of your life—who you are, what you are, however it is you've gotten to be where you are—God knows, God lures, God loves.

God invites us to cooperate with what God is doing in our own lives, and in the lives of others. This cooperation is not just a spiritual posture we carry in our hearts, but an active spiritual practice we embrace amidst the conditions in which we continue to know life and to know God. Two practices may be especially helpful: living in peace, and living in gratitude.

Living in Peace

In the Gospel according to John we learn of Jesus' parting gift: *Peace I leave with you; my peace I give to you. I do not give to you as the world gives.* Curiously, Jesus' peace had—and has—little to do with the absence of outward conflict. In Jesus' day, the surrounding atmosphere was one of hatred and rejection, where there was every prospect that Jesus' followers would meet an end that Jesus himself anticipated. *That* is the context in which Jesus gives his gift of peace: peace within, even when there is no peace without. What Jesus is talking about here is not *making* peace but *receiving* peace, the *gift* of peace. Or, at least the *offer* of peace. A gift becomes a gift only when the recipient receives it. Gifts require reception to become gifts, otherwise they are simply offers or prospects or promises or teases. The promise of Jesus' peace is ours for the having. It's a gift.

Receiving Jesus' gift of peace requires much attentiveness because there is so much that distracts us, so much that binds us, so much that distresses us, so much that takes our breath away. As you awaken to the dawn of a new day, make a practice of prayer that invites Jesus' peace to inform and infill you. You can carry this kind of breath prayer as you navigate through your day.

- breathe in Jesus' gift of peace and breathe out fear . . . or despair . . . or anxiety . . .
- breathe in Jesus' gift of peace and breathe out fear . . . or despair . . . or anxiety . . .
- breathe in Jesus' gift of peace and breathe out fear . . . or despair . . . or anxiety . . .

You might find it helpful to practice peace each day with the movement of your body, a way to walk, a way that you gesture or use your hands, a way of bowing or reverencing the Holy with your body. You might find it helpful *not* to multi-task, to do *one* thing at a time as often as possible. If you are listening to music, just listen. If you are sipping tea or watering the plants or petting the dog, do just that. Do one thing at a time, and do that as often as you can. Let the fragrances and aromas of life penetrate the deepest part of your being, where they can be savored.

You might find enormous help in a discipline of sitting in stillness. There may be a calming, centering phrase from the scriptures, especially from the psalms, for you to gently repeat under your breath to remind you of Jesus' gift of peace and to counter obsessive anxiety and compulsive thinking, such as:

> The LORD is my shepherd;
> I shall not be in want. (23:1)

> Show me your ways, O LORD,
> and teach me your paths. (25:3)

> I will bless the LORD at all times;
> his praise shall ever be in my mouth. (34:1)

> As the deer longs for the waterbrooks,
> so longs my soul for you, O God. (42:1)

> For God alone my soul in silence waits;
> from him comes my salvation. (62:1)

Bless the LORD, O my soul,
and all that is within me, bless his holy Name.
(103:1)

Draw on the gift of your senses. Practice gazing onto a serene landscape, a piece of art, or an icon, some object that you intentionally place in your line of vision at home or at work. The sense of touch may be useful with prayer beads, a rosary, a hand cross, or a spiritual medallion. A therapeutic massage may calm your body and balm your soul. Your sense of smell may be a powerful portal to remind you of the aroma of Christ's peace. The fragrance of fresh flowers, dried plants or herbs, or the scent of baking bread or stewing fruit may invite a helpful recollection. Listening to music may help bring internal orchestration to a cacophony of chaos in your soul. You may find grace in a shared practice of serenity—a twelve-step program or some other kind of intentional group who will listen, support, and cherish you because of some profound understanding that you and the group hold in common.

And lastly, you may need to make peace with yourself. Jesus calls us to love our enemies. If the truth be known, you actually may be your own first and worst enemy some days, and you can hate that part of yourself. The two of you—that part of you who knows better and that part of you who behaves worse—need to be on friendly speaking terms with each other. Unless we are reconciled to our own life, we miss the tools we need—buried in our own soul—to navigate life with meaning and integrity, and to relate to others with wisdom, courage, and mercy.

Receive that gift of peace, both for yourself and for others. When Jesus calls us to love our neighbors as we love ourselves, he is speaking *de*scriptively more than *pre*scriptively. That's simply the way it works. We love others the very way we love (or don't love) ourselves. Receive the gift of Jesus' peace, which will change your day, your life, and our world.

Living in Gratitude

It makes a remarkable difference to awaken to a new day as a gift, rather than as a given. Rising with the belief you may have only as much as one more day to know God, to love God, to serve God is to live eucharistically (with great thanksgiving). The reason we celebrate the Holy Eucharist—*Eucharist*, Greek for *great thanksgiving*—is not to create a sacred space on a Sunday morning amidst what otherwise is *normal* living. Rather, we celebrate the Holy Eucharist as a template and reminder of how to live our lives *all* the time, with deep gratitude. Gratitude consecrates our life and labor and makes us real.

Don't miss the opportunity to pray and savor your gratitude for what is so clearly good in life. Start small; start now. If you awaken to your alarm clock in the morning, be thankful that you can hear. If you can rise from your bed without assistance, be thankful. If fresh water is available, be thankful. If you can look outside your window, whether you see sunshine or rain, be thankful for your eyesight. If you can sit upright in a chair without having to be strapped in, be thankful. If you can drink a cup of coffee using your own hand, be thankful. If you can breathe without assistance, be thankful. Be thankful for everything you can in your own life. Likewise, express your gratitude to others every way, every time you can.

Say *yes* to the life you've been given, to the hand you've been dealt. Many people wake up to discover the script they've been handed in the play of life is not the part they thought they were trying out for. Living in gratitude is to accept how little of life is actually within our own control, an acknowledgment that God will be God, that it is God's world on God's time, and that we are God's creatures, cooperating in God's work, according to God's good pleasure. Living a *yes* is to accept the good gifts of life that actually *are* there, free of resentment for what is not there, or no longer there.

In God's providence, there is a reason why today is not tomorrow. We need the provisions of today to prepare us to receive the promises of tomorrow. In God's eyes, we shall always be *children of God*. Children are not developmentally ready to know everything at once. God knows what we do *not* know. In the meantime we wait until we are ready, until the fullness of time has come. God waits for us to be ready, for "the eyes of our hearts" to be enlightened. God also waits *with* us, until we are ready, like a parent or teacher waiting for a child to mature.

The psalmist speaks metaphorically, "Your word is a lamp to my feet and a light to my path." This particular source of light is not a megawatt arc beam, like one you might see shining down the runway of an airport. The light comes from an oil lamp, the light of a flickering wick that enlightens the path ahead, but probably only one step at a time. It is a small light, sufficient for illuminating what is next—but only that. God, who is light, will give us the light that we need and can bear, and will keep us in the dark for what we are not ready to see and know.

Spiritual direction for our future is informed by spiritual reconciliation with our past. Who we are, what we are, however it is we've gotten to be where we are, God knows, God lures, God loves. Practice the gift of Jesus' peace, which will change your day, your life, our world. Consecrate the miracle of your own life in thanksgiving. We live in a troubled and opportune time. Finding God's grace in the treasury of our own past, experiencing its redemption and blessing, gives us bearings to lean into God's future and to help others find the way, truth, and life promised by Jesus.

The Scribe Instructed in the Kingdom of Heaven

John Haughey, SJ

W HEN THE EPISCOPAL CHURCH gained a Presiding Bishop I lost a friend, and though I have seen Frank Griswold since then it has not been anywhere as often as I would like. When he moved to New York he left those of us who had grown close to him when he was Bishop of Chicago bereft of his presence. There are several things about him that I would like to elaborate on in this essay in his honor, as the memory of his character is unforgettable for me.

Thomas Aquinas began his monumental classic *The Summa Contra Gentiles* with the idea that "it belongs to the wise man to direct things." He was quoting Aristotle, who wanted to name the quality he had found in those who are skilled in directing and governing things well. I doubt, of course, that someone who is wise sees herself or himself as wise. That would be a bit pompous. But those who know them can say they are wise, and even they themselves, after the fact, might see their own wisdom. Frank Griswold was chosen to direct and govern in the Episcopal Church because those who knew him in lesser roles knew he was a wise man. That was the man I knew too.

I'm not quite done with Aquinas piggybacking on Aristotle since there is more that is relevant. Those two giants did not see wisdom simply as a matter of discrete acts. Wisdom becomes an art for those who develop the skills needed to know the ends of what they are governing and then fit their decisions to those ends. "The arts which govern others well are called master arts and those who acquire them master craftsmen." Vintage Thomas then takes over by noting that "the last end of each thing is that which is intended by the first author or mover of that thing, and the first author of the universe is an intellect . . . consequently the last end of the universe must be the good of the intellect, and this is truth."

When Frank Griswold and I had agreed on a date for lunch, it wasn't just his charm and attention and playful spirit that I looked forward to, although these were there. It was his intellect. As far as I could tell he read the wise and smart not to be wise and smart but simply to know. His *eros* was for knowledge. The good his intellect sought indefatigably was for knowledge of what is so, for what is true. Episcopacy can make one didactic, dogmatic, and doctrinaire. I never found him even remotely any of these. After ordering our lunch, we would enter together on the hunt to know because there was so much we didn't know and knew we didn't know. I don't want to convey the impression that we were two eggheads trying to sharpen our intellectual prowess. Rather, we were two brothers in Christ trying to ferret out a deeper understanding of the mysteries of Christ than the one we possessed.

Something else about Frank has made my affection and respect for him a slam dunk. It goes back to what Aquinas and Aristotle said about "ends." Frank underwent a yearly tune-up, so to speak, on these matters in his annual eight-day retreat based on the Spiritual Exercises of Ignatius Loyola. Ignatius was a master at enabling the retreatant to sort out the matter of ends and the choice of means to achieve those ends. From the get-go the notion called "the principle and foundation" is propounded to remind one that he "is created to praise, reverence and serve God." This is an insight into ends that is radical for one's self-understanding. The rest of the retreat then is aimed at deepening personal insight into this end for which each person has been created.

One ingredient of the efficacy of these exercises is the grace to come to insight into what deflects us from our end. The deeper part, however, is uncovering the pearl of great price, which is the awareness of the One who loves us unconditionally. One knows this from faith, of course, but there is the knowing that *knows* and the knowing that *does*. The truth that is done is known so much more deeply than the truth that is believed but not acted on. But I must avoid getting preachy here. What I as a Jesuit have found so helpful about making the Exercises, and found Frank loving about them too, is that in the course of the retreat truth becomes a person, "divine wisdom clothed in flesh," as Aquinas puts it in the same locus. If what fills the head can migrate to the heart, Christ becomes our wisdom.

The deeper themes of the Spiritual Exercises can be looked at in connection with the ordeal the Episcopal Church has been undergoing over the last few years, which I have watched from afar, as it faces questions and tensions. (We Catholics have not faced these questions as fully because of our different structure of authority; the ordeals of Catholicism tend to be of a different variety.) In the Spiritual Exercises the retreatant learns that following Christ is not a walk in the park. It is a commitment to follow Christ's way of taking on the burden of sin, including the sins of the communities of which one is a part. In the meditation on the Kingdom the retreatant hears Christ explain that "whoever wishes to join me in this enterprise must be willing to labor with me, that by following me in suffering he may follow me in glory." In other words, Jesus is saying to his disciple: *your path is not different from mine.*

Ignatius then expresses the disciple's commitment thus: "... it is my earnest desire and deliberate choice, provided only it is for Thy greater service and praise, to imitate Thee in bearing all wrongs and all abuse and all poverty, both actual and spiritual, should Thy most holy majesty deign to choose and admit me to such a state and way of life." As with any walk or life commitment, one only knows in the walking what was enfolded in the initial *yes.* I suspect Frank Griswold's *yes* and his prayer and reflection on that *yes* have led him on a path he could never have guessed he might walk.

I want now to focus on the commitment to imitate Jesus "in bearing all wrongs and all abuse." In my conversations with Frank one of the fruits of the presence of the Spirit I experienced was his forbearance, in the sense that he was always slow to judge, tolerant and patient with the limitations of others. It doesn't take much to see how this virtue would produce its own peculiar kind of suffering in his carrying out the responsibilities of Presiding Bishop. Has he been right, one could le-gitimately ask, in exercising forbearance, or should he be more authoritative? Admittedly, though asked from afar, this is still a good question. The more I think about this the more light I get from two parables, one about the tares and the wheat, the other about the seine-net that catches fish of every kind. In both cases there is the question of having to sort out the good from the bad, of separating that which is worthy of the kingdom and that which isn't. And in both cases there is the question of when to do this and who is supposed to do it. What is at stake in making these judgments is nothing less than the kingdom of God and its holiness.

I want to be more explicit about how these parables contain the wisdom of the Gospels and how they answer the questions I have posed here about Bishop Frank Griswold. The householder's servants are scandalized by the weeds that have encircled the good seed now grown into wheat, and they are passionate about uprooting them. They are instructed to let the weeds grow, fully aware that some enemy has sowed them (Matt. 13:28). In effect, they are not to attempt to anticipate the final judgment of God by their exclusion of those who give evidence of being unworthy of inclusion. There will be a time for the separation when the master of the harvest will gather the wheat into his barn, but for now let there be forbearance.

The parable of the net thrown into the sea being likened to the kingdom of heaven is equally enlight-ening for every one of us prone to what I might call "premature separationism." First, there is the question of the competence of those who would do the sorting out. Have they not, have we not, been hauled in because of the mercy of God? The sheep and the goats don't sort themselves out at the final judgment in Matthew; the eschatological judge does the sorting. So also in this parable it is "at the end of the age" that "the angels will go out and separate the wicked from the righteous" (Matt. 13:49).

Part of the issue here is the ubiquity of sinners; the kingdom of God is composed of saved sinners. Sinners who repent and the timing of their repentance as well as their conviction of what to repent of coming from the grace of compunction—all these are matters of the heart which only God can read. They are also a matter of timing. Both the when of repentance and the when of compunction are not chronologically predictable. *Kairos* timing, like God's thoughts and God's ways, is mercifully more lenient than *chronos* time. Hence the role of the virtue of forbearance in us and in our leaders.

One could legitimately ask here: What is the difference between the virtue of forbearance and the vice of irresponsibility that lets a thousand flowers bloom? A shepherd, after all, has to guide the flock. A bishop is an overseer of sheep, not an observer of them. If they meander hither and yon they will be prey to wolves. My question about forbearance—when is it defective and when excessive—is addressed by the cited parables in Matthew and the description of the role of the scribe. The parable teaches that if the scribe has been "instructed in the kingdom of heaven" he will show himself to be "like the head of a household who brings from his storeroom both the new and the old" (Matt. 13:52). This description fits Bishop Frank Griswold. He has been faced with new challenges, challenges my church has not yet been faced with on the same scale. I believe he has been faithful in finding in the storeroom of gospel wisdom both the treasures that have been there all along and new ways of understanding them for the present flock he guides.

Of course, the scribe who brings forth only the old from his storeroom will have much less of a problem than the scribe who has been instructed in the kingdom of heaven. The scribe instructed in the kingdom of heaven must discern the relationship between the old, the tried and true, and the new experiences and understandings of both him and his flock. The scribe who is merely church instructed is satisfied with handing on the deposit of faith in the same formulations in which it has been received. The scribe who has been instructed in the kingdom of heaven must be faithful not only to the old, the tradition, but to discerning that which is not yet formulated. He must take into account the word he hears in his heart, the word of God spoken to him in his interiority. This is where the new comes from, and discerning it is the challenge of such a scribe.

I spoke earlier of the Spiritual Exercises and their graces. As a Jesuit friend of Frank Griswold I see those graces present in his life and ministry. I thank this good scribe for his faithfulness and for bringing forth from his storeroom both the new and the old.

Reconciling Generations

M. Thomas Shaw, SSJE

T HE PRESIDING BISHOP is awesome," said sixteen-year-old Vanessa as we waited on a hot August day in the Miami Airport. We were on our way to El Salvador with other youth and mentors of our Diocesan Youth Leadership Academy to clear land for houses. Vanessa had recently returned from the Episcopal Youth Event in Kentucky with our primate, Frank Griswold, and 1,400 young people, lay adults, priests, and bishops from across the Episcopal Church.

"Why awesome?" I asked her.

"Because he did the white mouse dance for us at the airport when we were leaving the EYE," she replied.

"White mouse dance in the airport?" I questioned.

"Yeah," she went on, "so in one of his sermons he told us how in kindergarten he was chosen to be the head mouse with a white costume for the mouse dance. He practiced and he practiced but when it came time to perform his solo he was too scared to do it so he had to go back and be part of the chorus with the gray mice."

"And then?" I asked.

"*So,*" she said, looking at me like I *wasn't* very awesome, "when our group from Massachusetts met him in the airport we told him he had to do the white mouse dance right there. And he did it! The Presiding Bishop is very cool," she declared.

Frank Griswold is very cool, I thought to myself. He is a reconciler of generations. One of the reasons Christianity spread like wildfire around the Mediterranean during the first three centuries of the church's life is because the church was one of the few places in the Roman Empire where all people could gather. All the barriers in the Roman Empire that separated human beings were seen as alien to the Spirit of God as revealed in Jesus Christ. The church seemed to answer a deep longing in this very divided culture. The church, through the revelation of God in Jesus Christ and the life of the Holy Spirit, was the living reality of every human being made in the image and likeness of God. The church, all people living together with no barriers, in community, was how God had intended humankind to live from the beginning of creation.

"In community," states chapter 4 of the *Rule of the Society of St. John the Evangelist,* "we bear witness to the social nature of human life as willed by our Creator. Human beings bear the image of the triune God and are not meant to be separate and isolated. All of us are called by God to belong to communities of personal co-operation and interdependence which strive to nurture and use the gifts of each of us and to see that our basic needs are met."

On buses, at work sites, in Bible study classes, during individual spiritual direction, while hiking, or on confirmation retreats, teenagers almost always tell me that their deepest spiritual need is for community. They tell me that it is the community of the church that is most important to them during their adolescent years.

The longing of the early church, indeed, the longing of God, is their longing too. Like their ancestors in our faith, our teenagers seem to have the same sense that the barriers which divide us in twenty-first-century North American culture somehow impede them from becoming who they are meant to be and what God is calling the world to become. "Community is the biggest thing the church can give to me," writes Mary Elizabeth to me as she finishes her first year in college.

John, a young immigrant from Cape Verde, echoes Mary Elizabeth and goes on to say, "The church is a community for me. It's a community that shows love and care for me and for my family. The church community gives me peace and joy in my heart and it also helps get me closer to God." John, like most of our young people, knows that as one made in the image and likeness of God, he is fundamentally a person of peace, capable of great joy in a fragmented and disheartened world. He knows that in a culture like ours, which so often breeds alienation and isolation, deep intimacy with God is possible for him. John sees that it is the community of the church that opens to him this peace, joy, and intimacy.

This community our young people long for is not limited to a community of their peers; they want to be part of all of us. Youth groups, summer residential camps, large diocesan and national youth events, well-trained youth ministers, and ordained leadership that values and supports our young people are critical for their Christian formation. Nevertheless, our youth know that if they are to flourish in Christ they need the whole gathered family of a church community, including every age and generation.

This is what Andrea, a graduating high school senior, wrote to me: "Everyone needs support in their faith and it is also important to have role models who are unashamed in the way they live for Christ. I need someone who will hold me accountable for my actions because we can't always trust ourselves with our own accountability. I need fellowship with other young adults who understand my highs and lows . . . at the same time I need adults to share their wisdom and experience as well as listen to mine without judging."

When I reflect on what Andrea has written, those verses from St. Luke's Gospel concerning Jesus' formative years in Nazareth come to mind: how he grew strong and became filled with wisdom. How, I ask myself, did this happen? What were the boyhood experiences with his friends and family, the relationships with adults in and around Nazareth that sowed the seeds which grew and grew into the wisdom of the Beatitudes that he preached in his adult years? Who was he talking to as a teenager in his village of Nazareth or in the nearby city of Sephoris? What suffering did he see around him and experience himself in his years as a young person that allowed him to embrace the great cost of suffering as an adult? Which of his poor, or sick, or isolated neighbors was the invitation from God that drew him into the compassion of God that became the heart of his ministry to the outcast? For it couldn't all have come simply from his hearing of Scripture or from the religious education he received.

Because we believe in the incarnation, we have to believe that his strength and wisdom came from the particularity of his life: who he knew, what happened to him as a teenager, who he loved and disappointed, who encouraged him and, perhaps most of all, the mistakes he made as a young person. I wonder who helped him reflect on everything he experienced as a teenager. Who prayed with him and taught him to pray? Who were those women and men who not only spoke to him of God's love but whose actions in the daily life of Nazareth so eloquently bore witness to the words they spoke? Who wasn't frightened or threatened by the new ways God manifested in this teenager Jesus? Who was it that didn't judge the curious new things Jesus was saying? Who was it that encouraged those first stirrings in God's revelation? Who was the man or woman who didn't correct him or condescend to him or dismiss him?

If we want to be builders of community, if we, as adults, want to break down, in Christ, the barriers between generations, these are important questions for us. Each one of our young people is in Christ through baptism, and therefore, God is doing a new thing in them just as God was doing a new thing in Jesus the teenager. If we listen to Andrea, as adults, we have to be deeply aware of our own faith and yet ready to listen, without judging, to this bold God of ours who is creating fresh revelation of spirit through our young people. God calls our teenagers to be co-creators with God just as God calls us as adults to be creating with God. Therefore, to build the community our young people long for, we adults have to be asking ourselves again and again, what do *I* really believe? How am I living my faith? How do I pray? How important is worship to me? How am I letting myself be used by God for the redemption of the world?

Our teenagers want us to speak with integrity about

what we think we know of the life of faith, what we question, and how we have come to believe what we believe. They are depending on us, according to Andrea, for our wisdom and our experience. They want us, in turn, to listen to them with fresh ears knowing that all things are possible in God.

The community our teenagers and young adults desire is hard work for all of us. Building community has been hard work from the beginning. The oldest material in our New Testament canon is the letters of Paul. Paul's letters give clear witness to how difficult it is for generations, classes, those of different religious backgrounds, men and women, to be together in Christian community. Those struggling little communities spread out across Galatia, clustered together in Rome, in Corinth, Thessalonica, or Philippi, lived in constant debate and tension. It is the faithfulness of these emerging Christian communities to live in this tension that gives birth to the vitality of future generations in the church. These emerging Christian communities were in constant debate about worship, theology, ministry, and money, and they were influenced by personalities. Yet it is precisely this debate, engagement with one another about their life together in community, that uncovers the movement of the Spirit among them.

This is what it is like for a teenager who feels that the parish has given up on engaging their generation: "I personally need to be spiritually fed by the church. It may be my church in particular but I feel as though the youth are not accepted into the church family. Programs and events for the elderly are abundant, but support and excitement for youth is lacking . . . I would love to see my church work on addressing the teenage population.

This is the age when I personally have needed Christ's help the most, and it's also the age when other commitments and peer pressure convince youth that church is not important. My spiritual need is to see not only myself but others my age being spiritually fed by the church." When a congregation fails to engage a generation of young people—such as the young person just quoted—we not only deny the spiritual and pastoral care the teenager so desperately needs at a critical time in life, we also deprive the whole congregation of the Spirit-filled tension and engagement with them. And, this engagement is critical not only to the teenagers but to the growth and vitality of every other generation in the church community.

Worship is an example. Paul's letters reveal a great deal of engagement and tension in the church of the first century around the core of Christian life: worship. Who was the appropriate person to lead worship? How should the church pray together and share in the Eucharist? What was most important to worship? These were all explosive issues in Paul's time. The debate, at least partly, was caused because people from different religious backgrounds, different economic classes, and different genders were gathering together around the same table for the Lord's Supper. The issues raised were deeply felt by these early Christians. As tense as the engagement could be in these early communities, their faithfulness to staying together and engaging one another produced the heart of our worship today.

Our history provokes some questions. What did those early Jewish Christians bring to the debate on the nature of Christian worship? What did Gentiles, converts from mystery cults or state religions, add to the richness of early Christian worship? What did some have to give up so others would feel welcome at the table? Most of all, how were those early Christians transformed in Christ by engaging someone very different from themselves?

It is not uncommon for our young people, including those who regularly attend church on Sunday, to express dissatisfaction with the liturgy. "I don't usually find the guidance I am looking for in a regular Sunday service," writes one young adult. We know young people value worship, and not exclusively the worship they experience at large teen events with music, preaching, and teaching tailored for them. If they are included, the Sunday-by-Sunday worship is also important to them. Like all of us, our teenagers and young adults are looking for their place in creation. In spite of their own intense focus on who they are becoming, our teenagers are aware that they are creatures and that worship is vital to understanding the creature's relationship to the Creator.

What would older generations—some of us new to the Episcopal Church and some of us who have worshiped all our lives in this denomination—learn if we were to engage our young people every Sunday in our music, in our teaching and preaching, in our prayer? What glory could they give us? How might we ourselves be transformed? We don't know the answers to those questions until we risk engaging with our young people, those who come to church and those who don't come, in the planning and celebration of our liturgies.

It is not just in worship that God calls us to engage the newer generation of the church. Every part of our life in Christ—our theology, the mission and ministry of the church, our governance and our finances—might be deepened if we were to engage our young people. True reconciliation, between men and women, classes, races, and generations, means everyone moves to a new place.

"What do you have," I asked seventeen-year-old Caitlin, "that the church needs?"

"I can give," she replies, "my deep love, my unfathomable passion to be in communion and service to God. I hope the church can use my deep love for others and the presence of Christ I find in my prayer. I feel called to nurture and to lead. I feel called to be a spiritual leader through my speaking and my writing. I hope the church might use my perseverance and strength, even in the knowledge of my great weakness."

As an aging adult who is sometimes discouraged by my contribution and my generation's contribution in being agents of God's redemptive power in Christ in the world, I am inspired by Caitlin's response to me. I am inspired not only by what might be coming through young Christian women and men like Caitlin, but I also am inspired to dust off my cynicism and discouragement and open myself to the gift of hope God has given to me in baptism. Caitlin's generation is a source of the Spirit's renewing power for me: the stirring up of my baptismal gifts.

"Energy, enthusiasm, and a willingness and desire to learn more," says Sam, a junior in high school, in response to a question about what he has that the church needs. Answers like these from our young people diminish our fear and draw us into the boldness we read about in the church of the Book of Acts that is so clearly ours in baptism. But first we have to ask and then really listen.

Vanessa thinks Frank Griswold is awesome because

he is willing to engage her. He is willing to show a little of his goofy self in a dance in a crowded airport, but he also clearly heard her and all the other young people with whom he had shared the previous days. Not long after the Episcopal Youth Event, our primate wrote to his brother and sister bishops about the 1,400 young people from eighty-four dioceses in the Episcopal Church: "The depth and clarity of their faith and their eagerness to transform and heal our world was a powerful reminder of what it means to be members of Christ's body animated by the Spirit."

A Letter from Africa

Esther Mombo

Dear Bishop Frank,

Before the Lambeth Conference of 1998 your name was not widely known, particularly among Africans, but today many lay and clergy know the name of the primate of the Episcopal Church in the United States. Why is this? Surely one reason is the difficult issues you have had to deal with during your term of office.

I wish to send you this letter from Africa. Mine is the second largest continent on earth, measuring about 5,000 miles from north to south and about 4,600 miles from east to west. Africa's population is slightly less than 14 percent of the total world population. I know that the geography and demography of such a vast continent make it impossible for one person to write a letter reflecting the perspectives of its entire population. There are many others who remain silent; their voices are never heard.

First, I want to share with you some thoughts on the ecclesiology of Africa. Philip Jenkins, in *The Next Christendom: The Coming of Global Christianity,* writes:

> We are currently living through one of the transforming moments in the history of religion

worldwide. Over the past five centuries or so, the story of Christianity has been inextricably bound up with that of Europe and European derived civilizations overseas, above all in North America. Until recently the overwhelming majority of Christians have lived in White nations, allowing theorists to speak smugly, arrogantly, of "European Christian" civilization. Conversely, radical writers have seen Christianity as the religion of the "West" or, to use another popular metaphor, the global North.[1]

This view is sometimes used by historians of the Christian faith and church leaders as a form for employing moral blackmail and intimidation of the West.

According to the *World Christian Encyclopedia:*

> Some 2 billion Christians are alive today, about one-third of the planetary total. The largest single bloc, some 560 million people, is still to be found in Europe. Latin America, though, is already close behind with 480 million. Africa has 360 million, and 313 million Asians profess Christianity. North America claims about 260 million believers.[2]

Jenkins, who makes careful study of these figures, also makes this helpful projection:

> If we extrapolate these figures to 2025, and assume no great gains or losses through conversion, then there would be around 2.6 billion Christians, of whom 633 million would live in

Africa, 640 million in Latin America, and 460 million in Asia. Europe with 555 million would have slipped to third place.[3]

If one goes on using the numbers it is clear that there is a remarkable growth of Christianity in Africa. However, demography is not the only indicator for determining church growth, strength, and theological health. It is instead a secondary indicator and must be viewed in light of the current social, economic, and political realities.

Second, let us look at the social, economic, and political Africa. This story is not as positive as the ecclesiastical story because a very high proportion of the people live in extreme poverty; some of the countries are riddled with political instability and war. Further, most of the countries suffer from diseases such as malaria, which is resistant to many drugs. HIV/AIDS is decimating communities, undermining growth, and causing the loss of our human resources.

Also to be considered are environmental problems, including those resulting from global climatic change, which cause populations of the continent to continue to suffer—as do other parts of the world—from the devastating effects of floods, droughts, and other natural disasters.

As a theological educator who spends time with people both in Africa and beyond the continent, my experience of the varieties of African Christianity does not come simply from books or from hearing what is said by those in power. Rather, my experience comes from looking into the faces of individuals and hearing their stories. Here one finds the true picture and portrait of what is happening—beyond television images and statistics given by academics. The faces include those of grandmothers who host children orphaned by HIV/AIDS in their houses without pay or support, those of women who save from what little they have each week to build houses for each other and also feed the clergy of their churches. I hear the stories of men who work hard to see that they have piped water to their homes so that wives do not have to trek for long distances to look for water. I know of young people who form groups to work in fields to raise money for the church and to support themselves.

I also see the Africa where religious and political leaders are not facing up to or dealing with the life-threatening issues so long as they and their families are safe. I see the Africa where some politicians spirit money away to foreign accounts with brisk and deco-rous efficiency, and where bureaucrats don't give a damn about educational policy because their children are in universities abroad. I see religious leaders rejecting money that would have helped with the health of the members of their churches because their own children are not in those congregations but in the very countries they call evil or immoral. I see elites masquerading as entrepreneurs supplying bad seed to farmers and get-ting paid millions while the poor get no harvest. And so the cycle of hunger continues.

I am talking about two worlds of Africa. At one end, millions are slipping off into a life of hopelessness and death, while at the other the riches are piling up. As we discern the way forward for Africa, we must put on the lenses of the two worlds. We must move from a paternalistic savior interpretation of the cause and ef-fect kind to a more plain reality-pegged discourse. The

Christianities—that is, the ways of being a faithful Christian—that are being talked about for Africa, and used to challenge Christianities from other continents, need to be viewed through these two lenses.

There is need for a critical analysis of African Christianities and in particular African Anglican Christianity. If numbers are anything to go by, it is true that the number of Anglicans in some African countries is growing. Isichei has noted that more Anglicans go to church in Uganda than in England.[4] Of the 75 million Anglican members in 164 countries worldwide, Africa has 35.8 million. Over half of the world's Anglicans live in Africa. Looking at the numbers, the demographic figures are a sure indication that there is a growing Anglican community in Africa.

Having considered these numbers, we need to ask how committed are these vast numbers of individuals who are counted as Christians? For how many of them is faith just a superficial veneer? Even where church membership and attendance are high, it does not reflect the true situation. Often conversion comes quickly, but for many the roots remain shallow. To illustrate this, consider: Each year an anti-corruption group called Transparency International ranks the most corrupt nations. Kenya, which is stated as having a population that is 65 to 80 percent Christian, consistently appears as one of the most corrupt nations.[5]

But demography is not the only indicator for determining the theological or spiritual growth of the church in Africa. The growth and strength of the church are also measured by the way its teachings and practices are relevant in the society. We must look at how the teaching of the church is transforming those whom it is serving.

Desmond Tutu has observed that "African Christianity has suffered from a form of religious schizophrenia." There is an apparent split between what is taught and what is practiced. I can only speak of what I know: genocide, situations of rampant corruption, violence against women and children, to name some of the very telling examples. So a country can be very Christian and at the same time filled with tribal animosity and corruption in both the religious and secular sectors.

The African Anglican church continues to embrace numbers and outward forms of religion without translating this into the practice of the church. As a theological educator I confess that there has been a failure somewhere to produce leaders who are willing to understand the situation and deal with it. It is a great difficulty that among the hierarchy there is a deep suspicion that theological education kills the spirit. As a result we are getting leaders who are theologically illiterate but issuing threatening statements in the name of defending the church against modernity or progressive theologies. We are seeing superficial ways of dealing with issues that leave many wondering about the nature of the leadership of the church. It is a leadership that talks about servanthood but lives the opposite, choosing to position themselves as all-knowing and all-powerful in front of dependent lay congregations. This kind of leadership disempowers the laity in regard to education, politics, and even the sacraments. What the laity think about the issues facing them in all spheres does not come to the surface even as they seek ways of survival.

In defining his part of the Anglican Communion, an African Bishop said to me that we are theologically conservative but charismatic in worship. It would require an entire paper to unpack this statement; however, I would observe that though liturgy is central to Anglicanism, liturgies have been weakened in our African churches. It seems to me that the African Anglican Church has also embraced forms of worship in which being spiritual means being emotional in worship and saying the right things or using the right language. But the worship does not translate to very much in terms of how we live our Christian lives.

The church has grown, yes, but it seems little has changed from 1952, when Roland Oliver wrote that:

> the church has grown evangelically without cor-responding theological, liturgical and economic maturity. This "lamentable" situation needs to be addressed with all intentionality. There is an un-derstandable concern that under the stress of po-litical and social change, organized Christianity may start to disintegrate at the center while it is still expanding at the circumference.[6]

It is sad to note that Africa is treated as marginal in all spheres of world concerns except as a source of wealth for others and in matters of faith. But what faith? What practice? What theology? What church? These are the questions I am asking myself as I write this letter. But you may wonder if the situation is really that bad, Bishop Frank, because when you visited the continent you may have seen churches full of people rejoicing in the Lord. Yes, the churches are growing, but I am questioning the interpretation of that growth.

I have my take on the issues that put you in the limelight of the Anglican Communion, and on the responses from Africa in particular. I have argued elsewhere and believe it is still true that when we as leaders look at our continent and the problems we face we must conclude that the amount of time and energy devoted to these divisive issues is not well spent.

St. Francis of Assis prayed: "Lord grant that I may not seek to be understood but to understand." What seems to be lacking in leadership is understanding, empathy, acceptance of others, and searching and listening in order to build strength for all. A seminary student not long ago asked me if some of the leaders of the church live in the real world. He argued that the statements that some of the leaders make on issues that affect people show that they are detached from the real world, riding above it and seeing today's events in the perspective of a long sweep of history and projected into the indefinite future. But we need leaders to be in the real world and to be concerned, responsible, and effective in their ministry. In leadership one is obligated to be accountable for the process and for the results. There is need for mutual accountability between the leader and those who are led. Perhaps this is where there is misunderstanding on the events that have taken place in the Anglican Communion. It is my hope that we can learn from this current experience and thus strengthen our participation in the mission of God in the world.

As I said at the outset, this letter from Africa can't possibly reflect the perspectives of the entire African continent and all of our diverse peoples. Please know, however, that it is an honest word based on the experiences of one African woman. Know also of my prayers for you.

Your sister in Christ,

Esther Mombo

Notes

1. Philip Jenkins, *The Next Christendom: The Coming of Global Christianity* (Oxford: Oxford University Press, 2002), 1–2.
2. David B. Barrett, ed. *World Christian Encyclopedia: A Comparative Survey of Churches and Religions in the Modern World* (Oxford: Oxford University Press, 2001), 2–3.
3. Jenkins, 3.
4. Elizabeth Isichei, *A History of Christianity in Africa from Antiquity to the Present* (London: SPCK, 1995).
5. John Chesworth, "Southern Christianity and Its Relation to Christianity in the North Challenges to the Next Christendom: Islam in Africa," in Frans Wijsen and Robert Schreiter, eds., *Global Christianity: Jubilee of Chair of Missiology at Radboud University, Nijmegen* (New York and Amsterdam: Editions Rodopi, forthcoming Autumn 2006).
6. Roland Oliver, *The Missionary Factor in East Africa* (London: Longmans, 1952).

Laces Just Right:
Frank Griswold and the
Ethics of Reconciliation

William Danaher

My THOUGHTS ON Frank Griswold and reconciliation can best be organized around a story, a
story about an encounter, to be precise. In the spring of
1998, in the first months after his investiture as Presiding
Bishop, Bishop Griswold took part in a national conference for priests under the age of 35 hosted by Virginia
Theological Seminary. Showing remarkable generosity,
he spent three days with the three hundred priests gathered there, sharing with us something of the challenges
and joys of his own vocation. On this particular morning a group of us gathered around him between sessions, chatting informally. As we enjoyed the moment I
became aware that Tommy, a mentally retarded African
American man who worked in the kitchen at VTS,
was edging his way into the circle. While I was a student I had known Tommy. He usually kept to himself,
responding shyly to the greetings of the seminarians.
Now, however, he was moving forward determinedly.
Suddenly, he interrupted the conversation and in a loud

voice asked: "Would someone *please* tie my shoes?" No one moved. There was silence as everyone took measure of the speaker and the situation. Tommy looked off into the distance, waiting patiently, with the full expectation that, in good time, someone would have enough sense to tie his shoes. A feeling of paralysis ran through my body, which is my usual expression of panic—where others run screaming, I become catatonic. At that moment, I could no more have tied Tommy's shoe than walk on water. Then, in a very natural way Bishop Griswold knelt at Tommy's feet, looked up at him and smiled. "Tell me," he asked, "how do you like your shoe laces tied—tight, or loose?"

Over the course of that conference and throughout his episcopacy, I have been inspired by Bishop Griswold's deep love of theological reflection and commitment to spiritual growth. His sermons and addresses make plain that he believes the Christian life finds its center in *askesis*—the spiritual disciplines and practices that create characters that are shaped by the life of Christ, and in *theosis*—in the Spirit's dwelling within us in order to transform us through uniting us with God. Everything Bishop Griswold has taught, however, does not surpass the teaching contained in his living encounter with Tommy. For several years I have reflected on the dynamics involved in that encounter, particularly as related to the theology of reconciliation. Certainly, tying Tommy's shoes was a gifted improvisation of the gospel passages where Jesus washes his disciples' feet and where Jesus' feet are washed and anointed. Tommy came as Christ to our gathering, and Bishop Griswold welcomed him accordingly. Much more, however, lies beneath the surface of this encounter.

The Encounter in Depth

Tommy's request did not come from one unknown to us, but from one known and repeatedly denied hospitality. Tommy represented the marginalized, those excluded from our churches and communities. As an African American, Tommy was a member of a racial minority that continues to suffer discrimination, despite sporadic and uneven efforts to achieve equality. As mentally retarded, Tommy was a member of a minority that cannot compete on equal footing in a society in which the prevailing economic structures require intelligence, encourage autonomy, and reward productivity.

In addition to coming as Christ to us, then, Tommy was also a reminder of those members of Christ's family (Matt. 25:31ff.) we have discriminated against, neglected, or overlooked. While many factors enter into the persistence of racism and able-ism (as some call it) in our wider society, our church has perpetuated this twofold marginalization. Racism in the Episcopal Church is often camouflaged by pronouncements at diocesan and national conventions of racial reconciliation that lack programmatic content. Such abstract appeals for unity can actually serve to suffocate the cries for justice and equality.[1]

Further, our Prayer Book is written at a level only the educated in our society can read. In the language of sociology, the Prayer Book reflects the social capital of an economic and intellectual elite. In one breath, it reinforces divisions of class and capability as it proclaims the reconciliation of the world in Christ Jesus.

These forms of marginalization are symptomatic of farther-reaching sin and injustice. Just as a spider weaves a web that is the creation of its own genius and yet indistinguishable from all others, we are quick to weave the injustices of our society into the fabric of our particular Christian communities. In doing so, we deny our vocation to be, as Augustine conceived of it, an earthly image of the city of God (*civitas dei*): a community that is united by the love of God. Instead we retain the image of the earthly city (*civitas terrena*): a community that is consumed by a love that is self-aggrandizing, rapacious, born of violence.

Theologians have offered their own characterizations of this sinful love, defining it as the love of pride, of self-centeredness, of self-abasement.[2] Such characterizations are important, for to describe sin accurately enables an equally accurate description of grace. Moreover, as Marjorie Suchocki has observed, naming itself is an act of transcendence that can transform our consciousness, making us aware of the interrelatedness of all things.[3]

Rather than trying to isolate the psychological roots of what draws us away from the love of God, which lies beyond any simple description, it is important to identify the social expressions of sin in the desire to dominate and exploit others (*libido dominandi*). This desire, as Suchocki and Miroslav Volf suggest, issues in fundamental acts of violence and exclusion, often legitimized by unifying visions of a perfected self or society. These legitimizations are in turn predicated on self-deception: to be human is to experience an entrenched and unavoidable solidarity in sin, born of our participation in communities that embody violence and exclusion in one form or another.

The marginalization of African Americans, then, does not exist as a point of absurdity in an otherwise coherent and benevolent system. It is part and parcel of the predominant vision that conditions our self-understanding as a church and a nation, both of which grew in the soil of colonial imperialism. This vision is all the more poisonous in that it promises freedom, equality, and opportunity. As Enrique Dussel writes in *The Invention of the Americas* (1995):

> In the famed *triangle of death,* ships left London, Lisbon, The Hague, or Amsterdam with European products, such as arms and iron tools, and exchanged these goods on the western coasts of Africa for slaves. They then bartered these slaves in Bahia, Hispanic Cartagena, Havana, Port-au-Prince, and in the ports of the colonies south of New England for gold, silver, and tropical products. The entrepreneurs eventually deposited all that value, or coagulated human blood in Marx's metaphor, in the banks of London and in the pantries of the Low Countries. Thus modernity pursued its civilizing, modernizing, humanizing, Christianizing course.[4]

A similar solidarity in sin and systemic injustice lies behind the marginalization of the mentally retarded. Persons with disabilities occupy a more complicated terrain than do targets of racism, given that racism is entirely the product of social construction and bears no relation to capabilities. Disabled persons also suffer from stigmatizing values and injustice in the spheres of education, medicine, rehabilitation, social welfare policy and society at large. As Nancy Eiesland argues, there is a correlation between the bodies of persons with disabilities and their place within political bodies. Those who do not have "normal" bodies are often marginalized in the body politic and the body of Christ.[5]

Sadly, the body politic has proved more responsive to the plight of persons with disabilities than has the body of Christ, particularly with the passage of the Americans with Disabilities Act (1990)—the "emancipation proclamation," as Eiesland calls it, for people with disabilities.[6] The Act acknowledges that the 43,000,000 Americans who are disabled are "a discrete and insular minority who have been faced with restrictions and limitations, subjected to a history of purposeful unequal treatment, and relegated to a position of political powerlessness in our society."[7] Further, the Act mandated sweeping changes in policies and programs for persons with disabilities, so that they can live fulfilling and productive lives.

In contrast, despite affirmations of the Act by collective bodies, individual churches perpetuate acts of paternalism and social aversion, by segregating the disabled from the rest of the congregation, by discouraging them from taking leadership roles, and by designing worship services that make their contributions difficult and disruptive. Eiesland writes in *The Disabled God* (1994):

> Christ's body, the church, is broken, marked
> by sin, divided by disputes, and exceptional in
> its exclusivity. Church structures keep people
> with disabilities out; church officials affirm our
> spiritual callings but tell us there is no place
> for our bodies to minister; and denominations
> lobby to gain exception from the governmen-
> tal enforcement of basic standards of justice.

There is no perfect church as there is no "perfect" body.[8]

Bishop Griswold's encounter with Tommy, then, took place against a backdrop of oppression. And, as the spiritual leader of the Episcopal Church he could not claim innocence, for in taking on the mantle of authority he also accepted the yoke of our failings as members of the body of Christ. As Archbishop Rowan Williams writes, to be members of the body of Christ is to be in solidarity with those who are "wounded as well as wounding the church."[9] Further, to draw from one of the pastoral letters of Ignatius of Antioch (c.35–c.107), to be a bishop is to be a mirror of one's church.[10]

At the same time, given that Tommy was a capable kitchen worker, he probably could tie his own shoes. Any guile on his part does not diminish the oppression he and others have suffered; victims of oppression contend with the notion that their claims hinge upon their innocence rather than on the injustice of their situation.[11] Nonetheless, in addition to expressing the simple need for attention or care, it seems likely that Tommy's request signaled that he had appropriated the role of the stigmatized. After years of social interactions with non-stigmatized persons, he knew this role well enough to take the lead in his dramatic encounter with the Presiding Bishop, hence his confident expectation that, in due time, his shoes would be tied.[12]

What was remarkable in this encounter, then, was not that Tommy asked that his shoes be tied or that Bishop Griswold tied them. However, by asking how Tommy wanted his shoes tied—tight or loose?—Bishop Griswold showed that he was willing to enter into a risky situation fraught with the potential for misunderstanding and perhaps embarrassment in the hope that he could somehow break through the mutual isolation between them created by sin and injustice. If it is true, as suggested earlier, that the relation between stigmatized and non-stigmatized is a kind of play in which actors inhabit assigned roles in order to avoid the discomfort and tension that come when the stigmatized try to pass for, or are mistaken as, "normal," then Bishop Griswold's question was an attempt to transform his role, and the play, into something greater, into another play scripted after Christ's redemption.

His question displayed empathy: the ability to feel what another is feeling through entering imaginatively into their world and experience. This empathetic move was composed of a movement *inward*—in that he remembered what it was like to have his shoes tied and how important it was that they be tied comfortably, and a movement *outward*—in that he had to imagine that Tommy also would have such a preference. His question also displayed compassion: the capacity to participate in another's suffering. In doing so, he entered into the spirituality of the moment, making his encounter with Tommy an opportunity for love and worship. By this I mean that the ultimate context for his encounter was neither the backdrop of oppression nor the *personae* each inhabited, but the movement out of oneself (*ekstasis*) on account of an apprehension of God through the very particulars of Tommy.

This was not worship in the sense of cleaving to a higher beauty or greater good so that the differences between him and Tommy faded from view. Rather it was the resolution to see and welcome Tommy's otherness, with the confidence that God has revealed himself in the world precisely in this way, as an "other" who was loved and rejected, welcomed and crucified. The ground of his question, of his love and worship, and of the otherness of Tommy, then, was Jesus Christ, the "Other."

Reconciliation and the Paschal Mystery

Theological reflection on reconciliation often begins with Paul's proclamation in 2 Corinthians 5:18–19: "All this is from God, who reconciled us to himself through Christ, and has given us the ministry of reconciliation; that is, in Christ God was reconciling the world to himself, not counting their trespasses against them, and entrusting the message of reconciliation to us" (NRSV). To be sure, the church stands or falls on the truth proclaimed in this passage. As John de Gruchy has argued, it provides important teaching on the theology of reconciliation viewed through the prism of the cross: The root of the Greek word for reconciliation, διαλασσομαι, is a compound of αλλασσω, "to exchange," which in turn derives from αλλαοσ, meaning "the other." Thus, the passage teaches that reconciliation entails the sense of exchanging places with "the other," and therefore being in solidarity with, rather than against, "the other." The idea of vicarious representation, then, lies at the heart of reconciliation so construed:

> Reconciliation literally has to do with the way in which God relates to us, the human "other," and in turn with our relationship to "the other," whether understood as an individual person or a group of people. It has to do with the process

of overcoming alienation through identification and in solidarity with the "the other," thus
making peace and restoring our relationships.
Reconciliation has to do, if we may put it so
colloquially, with God making us friends.[13]

De Gruchy's theological grammar resonates with
Bishop Griswold's encounter with Tommy, and indeed,
connects the idea of reconciliation to the understanding about Christ as the "other" that grounds our respect
for "others." In addition, particularly in the aftermath of
violence, this cruciform vision of reconciliation attests
to Christ's power to absorb and transcend the violence
done to him. In this way, the cross is God's judgment on
the destructive desire to dominate (*libido dominandi*)
that pervades human social relations. Within the realm
of criminal justice, as Christopher Marshall has argued,
the cross destabilizes human attempts to render retributive justice, particularly when viewed alongside Jesus'
revision of the biblical injunction of "an eye for an eye"
(Matt. 5:43–48). The justice established on the cross is
one that is satisfied only by forgiveness and restoration. Thus, "divine justice may entail punitive sanctions
against wrongdoers," but "it does not rest content with
punishment, for it is fully satisfied and fully vindicated
only when healing and repair occur."[14] Within the realm
of political justice, as N. T. Wright has argued, the cross
represents the "victory of God" over the powers of this
world, a victory that has already been accomplished on
our behalf, a reconciliation that is complete and real, if
not yet fully revealed in the here and now.[15] To work for
reconciliation, then, represents the determination to live
by the politics of this new rule of God.

This cruciform vision of reconciliation, however, has difficulty accounting for the fact that reconciliation is often chaotic and fragmentary, full of false starts and disillusioning failures. It cannot account for the way we are called to work for reconciliation even in circumstances that seem impossible, where we contend with obstacles that seem to render any positive response impossible, where the structures of our own sin and injustice have locked us into a role and a play that feel set in stone.

This was the situation Bishop Griswold found himself in with Tommy, and yet he was able to transform the encounter by accepting his limitations and hoping for some glimpse of the power that reconciles us all. For in that encounter, he showed himself willing to claim a "reconciled identity," an identity formed by the acceptance of Christ's judgment and forgiveness.[16] As Archbishop Rowan Williams writes in *Resurrection* (2002), this identity is made possible by the cross, but it is realized when we meet the risen Jesus.

As the resurrection accounts in the Gospels reveal, the risen Jesus is also the crucified Jesus. Indeed, it is by his wounds that the disciples recognize him (John 20:20; Luke 24:39–40). But the risen Jesus represents an unexpected departure from the story as it is usually told. Now, instead of the finality of death and violence, there is an unexpected transformation—a "transition," in Williams's words, from the "destructively familiar" to the "creatively strange."[17] The disciples enter the strangeness of this new story through their own reconciliation with Jesus, whom they have denied and abandoned, who has been the victim of the violence that pervades earthly existence, a violence in which they have colluded.

This paschal vision of reconciliation is most evident in those accounts where the disciples have engaged in explicit acts of repudiation and violence, such as Peter's breakfast with the risen Christ, in which Jesus asks him three times, "Do you love me?" (John 21:15–19) and Jesus' confrontation with Saul, who faces the question, "Why do you persecute me?" (Acts 9:4). In both cases, the offenders encounter the risen Lord and receive—in the same moment—judgment and mercy. The risen Lord, who stands in solidarity with all victims through his cross, vindicates the oppressed and yet saves the oppressors, thus initiating a new way to transcend the domination and diminution that characterize human society. Instead of placing the victims over the oppressors, which only changes the roles but not the script, Jesus' reconciliation presents an invitation to live an entirely new life, one in which the past loses its power to control us, though it is not forgotten. Rather, through graced confrontation and absolution the past is redeemed, making a new future possible.

In other resurrection accounts—on the road to Emmaus and Jesus' meeting with the women at the tomb— the work of reconciliation is more implicit, happening in meetings with a stranger to whom the disciples extend hospitality (Luke 24:29) and with a stranger who brings comfort (John 20:15). These other accounts are no less moments of reconciliation, even if the process of confession and absolution lies beneath the surface of the discourse. For in these moments, the disciples meet the Lord who reconciles that which appears to our eyes diametrically opposed—heaven and earth, time and eternity, life and death, sin and salvation, peace and justice, judgment and forgiveness. Reconciliation does not begin with Jesus' work on the cross, then, but begins in Jesus' person—by his incarnation as Emmanuel ("God with us"). Jesus *is* the reconciliation of God and humanity, even before he does any *work* of reconciliation. Thus, the resurrection of Jesus follows God's character as creator, bringing forth out of nothing *(ex nihilo)* a new creation that gracefully disorients us.[18] Jesus is not, as the disciples had assumed, a "dead friend" but a "living stranger" with whom they must become reacquainted.[19] Now, they meet Jesus in the victim and in the stranger.

Reconciliation is evident even in the accounts of the empty tomb, in which Jesus' resurrected presence is manifested by the physical absence of the body. For these accounts strip away any pretense of controlling the narrative—part of developing a reconciled identity requires the surrender of attempts to control the role or the script of the play the disciples inhabit. If Jesus is not found in the empty tomb, he can be anywhere, at any time, in anyone. The disciples are no longer actors in a tragedy, in which a tragic figure meets his end heroically battling forces that eventually overwhelm him. Precisely what dramatic genre they now inhabit is hard to characterize; it has the improvisational elements of comedy, but elements of tragedy still remain. Many of the disciples will meet a similar end as the figure of the cross becomes imprinted on their lives, but the resurrection assures them that the drama in which they now participate is only just beginning.

Another benefit is that the resurrection accounts depict the experience of reconciliation from *inside* the paschal event, from the perspective of disciples with all their gifts and flaws on display. The resurrection accounts therefore treat reconciliation not so much as an accomplished reality that stands beyond our current experience but as an unfolding mystery and a drama that continually surprise us as we work out our salvation in Christ. For this reason, attempts to transfer the template of reconciliation from one context to another will always encounter stiff resistance. Like forgiveness, reconciliation must be personal and particular. Further, when viewed in light of the paschal mystery, reconciliation begins with a new identity created out of our own encounter with the risen Lord and ends with the resolve to live in a new kind of community.

Finally, this reconciled identity lies at the heart of the church's witness and worship. In terms of its witness, the church has no other option than "to live in penitence, in critical self-awareness and acknowledgement of failure," constantly remembering its "failing *as* a community to *be* a community of gift and mutuality."[20] To partake in this penitence requires that we tell the stories of those we have oppressed, so that we might corporately live into the reconciliation to which we are called. This recounting of the past will be painful and, in the eyes of some, unnecessary, given our penchant to deny the past rather than confront it. In terms of its worship, however, the church has in the Eucharist an example of a past that can also be transformed into a source of new life and a new identity. Thus, "when the church performs the Eucharistic action it *is* what it is called to be: the Easter community, guilty and restored, the gathering of those whose identity is defined by their new relation to Jesus crucified and raised, who identify themselves as forgiven."[21]

Worship and Reconciliation

Of course, throughout our lives, we remain sinners "of God's redeeming."[22] Faithfulness to our reconciled identity demands that we continue to recognize all the ways we remain mired in structures of sin and injustice, even as we try to receive the gift of God's reconciliation with our whole being and to realize it in our communities. For now, the new creation we celebrate in the Eucharist is perfected only in worship, and it is most often experienced in fragments of community where the love of Christ somehow manifests itself in transformative moments, in encounters with victims and strangers. When we live into the spirituality of these encounters, however, and work for reconciliation in our own contexts and communities, we receive from his fullness "grace upon grace" (John 1:16). This is precisely what Frank Griswold was doing when he knelt and tied Tommy's shoes. When he did so, he probably did not ponder for a moment the theology of reconciliation. But his action on that spring morning grew out of a deep appropriation of a reconciled identity cultivated through prayer and companionship with Jesus. For this, his life in Christ, I am grateful.

Notes

1. For an important and heartbreaking view of this tendency, see Gardiner H. Shattuck, Jr., *Episcopalians and Race: Civil War to Civil Rights* (Lexington: The University Press of Kentucky, 2000).

2. Here I refer in passing to the different harmatologies of Richard Hooker (pride), Reinhold Niebuhr (self-centeredness), Susan Nelson Dunfee (self-abasement). This is a far-from-exhaustive list, but it helps reinforce my prejudice against

essentialist descriptions in theology as well as the heuristic appropriateness of naming all that separates us from the love of God.

3. See Marjorie Suchocki, "Original Sin Revisited," *Process Studies* 20, no. 4 (Winter 1991) http://www.religion-online.org.

4. Enrique Dussel, "The Invention of the Americas: Eclipse of 'the Other' and the Myth of Modernity," M. D. Barber, trans. (New York: Continuum, 1995), 122–23. Quoted from Miroslav Volf, *Exclusion and Embrace: A Theological Exploration of Identity, Otherness, and Reconciliation* (Nashville: Abingdon, 1996), 59–60.

5. Nancy L. Eiesland, *The Disabled God: Toward a Liberatory Theology of Disability* (Nashville: Abingdon, 1994), 22.

6. Ibid., 19.

7. Americans with Disabilities Act, 101st Cong. (1990), 2nd sess., 3. *U.S. Statutes at Large*, vol. 104, 329. Quoted from Eiesland, *Disabled God*, 56.

8. Eiesland, *Disabled God*, 108.

9. Rowan Williams, "Making Moral Decisions," *The Cambridge Companion to Christian Ethics*, R. Gill, ed. (Cambridge: Cambridge University Press, 2001), 11.

10. Ignatius of Antioch, "The Epistle to the Magnesians" in *Early Christian Writings: The Apostolic Fathers*, M. Smith, trans., A. Louth, ed. (New York: Penguin, 1987), 71.

11. See Christine Gudorf, *Victimization: Examining Christian Complicity* (Philadelphia: Trinity Press International, 1992), 60, passim.

12. See Erving Goffman, *Stigma: Notes on the Management of Spoiled Identity* (New York: Simon & Schuster, 1963), 10–11. For an important discussion of the insights and limitations of this analysis, see Eiesland, *Disabled God*, 58–61.

13. John W. de Gruchy, *Reconciliation: Restoring Justice* (London: SCM Press, 2000), 51.

14. Christopher D. Marshall, *Beyond Retribution: A New Testament Vision for Crime, Justice, and Punishment* (Grand Rapids: Eerdmans, 2001), 94.

15. See N. T. Wright, *Jesus and the Victory of God* (Minneapolis: Fortress, 1996), 610 and passim.

16. Rowan Williams, *Resurrection: Interpreting the Easter Gospel*, Revised Edition (Cleveland: Pilgrim Press, 2002), 79.

17. Ibid., 69.

18. Ibid., 17.

19. Ibid., 74.

20. Ibid., 48–49.

21. Ibid., 52.

22. See The Book of Common Prayer, 483: "a sinner of thine own redeeming."

Afterword

George L. W. Werner

THE GOSPEL OF JESUS CHRIST is impractical and often conflicts with what might be thought of as the conventional wisdom. Too often conventional wisdom is anything but wise: Conventional wisdom held that the longed-for Messiah would be a king or a general leading massive armies that would strike down the enemy and conquer the world. As it turns out, the symbol of the church is not a sword but a cross, a place to receive the pain of the world. On the night before Jesus was crucified, he called us to love one another. From that cross, Jesus forgave even those who were crucifying him. The summary of the law tells us to "love our neighbor even as we love ourselves."

We live in a difficult moment of history. Remarkable technologies permit us to view instant images from anywhere in the world and to communicate with most anyone, anywhere. Sometimes we use these instruments for the good of God's children. However, too often they have become the means of spreading dread and enmity: dread meaning the kind of fear that paralyzes and renders us unable to become a community, and enmity meaning the kind of cancerous hatred that metastasizes in our hearts and brains and our very souls.

Paul, once the quintessential party man—zealous to the point of being a zealot—discovered a better way. In Galatians, he turns his back on party spirit, praying "May I never boast of anything except the cross of Our Lord Jesus Christ" (6:14). In Colossians he implores the Colossians to "Bear with one another, if anyone has a complaint against another, forgive each other; just as the Lord has forgiven you" (3:13). To a world that cried for a warrior as their Messiah, Paul declared, "put on the breastplate of faith and love, and for a helmet the hope of salvation" (1 Thess. 5:8).

To hunger and thirst for reconciliation is to challenge conventional wisdom. It requires the humility to understand that we may not be as wise as we think. It requires a willingness to do more than what seems to be fair. It requires the courage to be vulnerable, to put oneself in the way of danger and to risk costly love.

In the fifteenth chapter of Luke, the Evangelist responds to the rebukes of the Scribes and Pharisees with three parables: The Lost Sheep; the Lost Coin, and the Lost Sons. My biblical mentor has taught me to seek the scriptural stories of "unexpected demonstrations of costly love." We see such costly love again in Luke 19 when, on his way to Jerusalem and Calvary, Jesus risks the wrath of village leaders to reconcile with Zaccheus, the worst sinner in Jericho.

Reconciliation is not simply a worthy concept; we live it. Over more than forty years of priesthood, I have seen dramatic changes in those who take the risk of reconciliation. One such was a young woman who appeared as a walking corpse when I met her. Her eyes were devoid of light and life and her voice was flat. After months of apparently fruitless counseling, she read an article on forgiveness. She felt compelled to seek reconciliation with her emotionally abusive father. After their encounter those of us who knew her could not believe what we were seeing. She seemed taller, animated, bursting with joy. Her eyes glowed and radiated. Her voice was musical. Bitterness and anger were gone and she appeared like an Angel sent from God.

This collection of essays on reconciliation is a particularly fitting tribute for Frank Griswold. It has been an often stormy nine years. It has been a time during which one could easily be tempted to stop thinking about reconciliation and forgiveness and turn instead to revenge and self-pity. However, never once in these years, in conversation private or public, have I ever heard the Presiding Bishop stray from his passion for reconciliation and conversation. I have never heard him breathe a word about revenge. As his colleague for six years of our bicameral General Conventions I am very deeply aware of what he has given to the Episcopal Church as he has strived to fulfill the words of Paul: "Above all, clothe yourselves with love, which binds everything together in perfect harmony" (Col. 3:14).

Afterword

Peter James Lee

R ECONCILIATION IS A MAJOR THEME of the ministry of Frank Griswold. But it is not a program and not a strategy. Rather, throughout his years as Presiding Bishop and Primate, his attention to reconciliation has been grounded in a spirituality of the cross that acknowledges the depth of human pain and alienation and the transcendent power of the reconciling love of God in Christ that enters that pain and offers the promise of healing.

Among those many who love Frank Griswold, a story (probably apocryphal) is told that demonstrates his theological integrity. A staff member came into his office one day and announced excitedly, "Bishop, we've just received a $50,000 gift to be used any way you wish!" Griswold responded, "That's wonderful. We must make sure we honor the Incarnation." Staff member: "But how will we spend it? What do you want to do?" Griswold: "Whatever we do, we must honor the Incarnation."

The staff member wanted a programmatic decision from a manager or a politician. Griswold is neither. His deep faith is grounded in the reconciling love of God, not expressed in well-managed programs.

Frank Griswold planned liturgies for the House of

Bishops in the years before he was elected Presiding Bishop. His colleagues remember affectionately the "Griswold pause" in reading the psalms in the daily office. He insisted that the often-ignored rubric in The Book of Common Prayer's instruction for the reading of the psalms be honored: "a distinct pause should be made at the asterisk" (583).

The psalms are at the heart of Frank Griswold's spirituality of reconciliation. He knows them intimately through a lifetime of reading the Daily Office. As Ellen Davis's essay counsels, on the day of trouble, Frank Griswold has been able to rivet his attention on God's goodness, because he has taken his troubles—and the world's grief—to the foot of the cross and experienced the goodness of God celebrated in the psalms.

Frank Griswold's concern for reconciliation is expressed in a profound regard for "the Other." The Other may be a stranger, even an enemy, but in Griswold's spirituality the Other is often a form through which the utterly transcendent and holy God makes God's Self present to human beings. Griswold has been criticized in some conservative circles for acknowledging the pluriform character of truth. His respect for the Other, his honoring of many dimensions of truth, actually reveals an orthodox reverence for the sovereignty of God and the impossibility of any human claim to possess all truth. Denise Ackerman writes of an "embodied spirituality of reconciliation." In the humble and prayerful approach to Scripture we find in Frank Griswold, in his tireless efforts to call the church to a holy regard for "the Other," we have experienced such an embodied spirituality.

His spirituality is not unlike that of the early fathers and mothers of the desert of whom he often speaks. A typical Griswold teaching might begin, "As Anthony the Anchorite wrote so many years ago ..." In the tumult of the fourth century, when so much was changing, spiritual explorers went into the deserts of Egypt, Syria, and Palestine to experience God in the stillness of prayer. Frank Griswold has led his church in a time of tumult. Perhaps his lasting contribution is his example of dedication to reconciliation forged in the silence of prayer.